Life, Liberty **&**
The Pursuit of
HOLLYWOOD

Other Books by Michael B. Druxman

Fiction

Dracula Meets Jack The Ripper & Other Revisionist Histories
Once Upon A Time In Hollywood: From the Secret Files of Harry Pennypacker
Shadow Watcher
Nobody Drowns In Mineral Lake

Non-Fiction

My Forty-Five Years In Hollywood And How I Escaped Alive
Family Secret (with Warren Hull)
The Art of Storytelling
The Musical: From Broadway To Hollywood
One Good Film Deserves Another
Charlton Heston
Merv
Make It Again, Sam
Basil Rathbone: His Life and His Films
Paul Muni: His Life And His Films

Stage Plays (*The Hollywood Legends*)

Clara Bow
Chevalier
Flynn
Gable
Jolson
Lombard
Nelson and Jeanette
Rathbone
Tracy
Orson Welles

Other Stage Plays

Hail on the Chief!
Putz
The Summer Folk

Screenplays

Barry & The Bimbo
Black Watch / The Cavern
Charla
Cheyenne Warrior
Cheyenne Warrior II / Hawk
Ghoul City
Matricide
Ride Along
Sarah Golden Hair
The Summer Folk
Uncle Louie

Life, Liberty & The Pursuit of HOLLYWOOD

More of My Wacky Adventures in Tinseltown

by Michael B. Druxman

BearManor Media
2013

Life, Liberty & The Pursuit of Hollywood:
More of My Wacky Adventures in Tinseltown

© 2013 Michael B. Druxman

All rights reserved.

For information, address:

BearManor Media
P. O. Box 71426
Albany, GA 31708

bearmanormedia.com

Typesetting and layout by John Teehan
Cover photo: Elisa Ferrari

CASABLANCA serigraph © Melanie Taylor Kent, LTD.

Published in the USA by BearManor Media

ISBN— 1-59393-738-5
978-1-59393-738-6

For
Missy, Annie, Cody, Jasmine, Gizmo, Kate,
Chester, Charlie (2), Ginger, Skeezicks, Harvey,
Roscoe, Fred, Sean, Lady, Duchess, Fang, Duke,
Whiskers, Pixie, Dorcas, Whiskers, Daffy, Lucy,
Rusty, Blackie (2), Bonnie, Pocket Pal, and
all my other little friends who have given me
unconditional love and happiness
throughout my life.

We will meet again at the Rainbow Bridge.

Table of Contents

Preface vii

1 The Outsider 1
2 The Employee 9
3 The Actor 13
4 The Actor-Director 21
5 The Producer-Director 31
6 Limbo 37
7 The Publicist 43
8 Rock Hudson 49
9 Gale Gordon, Composers & Directors 53
10 Comedians & Other Clients 63
11 Dracula, Clemenza & Charles 71

   Photo Section 80

12 Jane Fonda, George Raft & Other Non-Clients 97
13 Michael Ansara 107

14	Flubs & Practical Jokes	117
15	Difficult & Unusual Clients	123
16	Musings About Actors	131
17	Musings About Writers	141
	Photo Section	149
18	Writing & Roger Corman	165
19	The Ambush	175
20	Pet Projects	183
21	The Publisher	195
22	Autograph Shows	203
23	Surviving in Austin	211

Preface

WHAT IS THE SINGLE, most important asset that an aspiring screenwriter, director, actor or any other person wishing to scale the moat-surrounded, alligator-filled, walls of Hollywood should possess?

Talent?

Having some certainly helps, but that's not the answer. There are plenty of folks with a bare minimum of that gift who make very good livings in the film business. Just look at some of the movies out there these days and you'll see what I mean.

Family Connections?

A definite plus, yet there are plenty of folks, like myself, who began with no connections whatsoever and developed their own.

Give up?

The correct answer is *TENACITY*.

It took me ten years of trying before my first screenplay sale…and by the time that happened, I'd already been working in the motion picture business (primarily as a self-employed publicist) for almost twenty-five years. After that, the sales and assignments kept coming.

With patience, a bit of luck and being prepared to take advantage of opportunities when they came my way, I was able to achieve my life-long dream to write and direct movies.

You can dream…or you can do. I did.

I was never a big fish in the Hollywood pond, but I did swim and play with the big fish…none of whom ate me.

And that's what this story is about.

Thank you for buying (*I hope*) this book. I trust that you will enjoy reading and learning from it.

However, if you have not already read my 2010 memoir, *My Forty-Five Years in Hollywood…And How I Escaped Alive*, I strongly suggest that you set this book down for the moment, go to your computer and order that volume from Amazon or elsewhere immediately.

If you don't do that, I fear that there will be several instances in the reading of this more recent book that you will be wondering, perhaps aloud, *"How the hell did he do that?"* or *"Where did that person come from?"*

The answers to those and other earth-shattering questions can be found in my first memoir…*which is why you should read it first.*

In 1992, actor Michael Caine wrote *What's It All About?*, one of the most entertaining show business autobiographies I've ever read. Then, in 2010, he came out with a second memoir, *The Elephant to Hollywood*.

Though also an enjoyable read, the problem with his later book is that virtually the first half of it was an abridged duplication of the initial work. Readers of that first book, looking to hear Caine's "further adventures," were a bit "ripped-off," forced to read perhaps 150 pages of reprise before the actor got to the years 1993-2010.

I didn't want to do that with my second memoir, which I'm writing a little over two years after the first one was published.

You may wonder why, after only two years, I've written a second memoir. Except for writing a collection of short stories (*Dracula Meets Jack the Ripper and Other Revisionist Histories*), *Nelson and Jeanette*, a two-person stage play about Nelson Eddy and Jeanette MacDonald and *Rathbone*, a one-person play about Basil Rathbone, plus having my biography of Basil Rathbone republished after thirty-five years out-of-print, not that much has happened to me since I wrote "The End" on that first book. True, I've had a lot of other books published in paperback and on Kindle since then, but those were stage and screenplays that had already been written over a period of many years.

A good story is a terrible thing to waste.

Once *My Forty-Five Years in Hollywood…And How I Escaped Alive* had been sent off to the printer, I realized that there were many stories, both humorous and life lessons, that I had neglected to tell in that work, either because I had momentarily forgotten them or because you can only tell just so much in one book.

But, was there enough new material for an entire new book?

I started writing down the stories and, while doing that, not only did more stories emerge from the depths of my 72 year-old memory, but I also discovered interesting things about myself that perhaps I'd glossed over in the first book.

Soon, I had written well over two hundred pages, and here we are.

I have done my best to avoid Michael Caine's mistake. My guess is that perhaps ninety percent of the material in this book is totally fresh, and the only times that I have repeated stories from my earlier memoir are when I felt that the new material needed to be put into context.

So, I repeat (*and not for the last time*), if you haven't done so already, please read that first memoir first. If you do, then I can virtually guarantee that you will enjoy this book—its miscellaneous musings and snapshots—much more.

That said, come with me now as I relate my encounters with Hollywood's rich and famous…and also myself.

1

The Outsider

I DON'T THINK I WAS EVER "AN ARTIST".
Talented?
Yes.
Artistic?
Definitely.
But, willing to starve in a garret for my art?
Absolutely not!
I liked my creature comforts too much.

By "creature comforts," I mean having a nice place in which to live, not having to agonize over where my next meal was going to come from, being able to drive a decent car instead of taking a bus and having extra money in my pocket. I would also prefer having a dog or cat for a pet, rather than a herd of cockroaches.

A cockroach won't even come when you call it.

As my mother used to say, "I don't want to have to worry whether I can afford a roll of toilet paper."

My father, who came from a poor, working class immigrant family, put it another way: "If you're going to go, then go first class."

Dad really believed in "first class". He was a snappy dresser, and if he saw an actor wearing a piece of clothing he liked in a movie, he would have to have it. After he saw a vest that Edward G. Robinson was wearing in *Little Caesar*, Dad sent his tailor to that gangster classic six times, so that he could copy it. The same thing happened when he admired a topcoat that William Holden wore in *Sunset Boulevard*. An exact copy of that garment went into Dad's closet.

I still have both of those pieces of clothing packed away somewhere.

I've never needed "first class". When I fly, unless it's on a business trip when somebody else is paying for the ticket, I go "coach".

Actually, celebrated independent producer Roger Corman, who gave initial career breaks to everybody from Jack Nicholson to Ron Howard to Martin Scorsese, and for whom I've written many screenplays, also flies "coach," so I'm in good company.

Like you, I've heard and read all the stories about the financial hardships and frustrations that many of our most esteemed actors endured while trying to get their first break in the entertainment business, and I respect and admire them for that.

Rejection, it's been said, is good for the soul and makes for a more sensitive artist. The more rejection…the more sensitive the artist.

Rejection can also result in an angry artist, but I'll address that later.

I've had to endure many rejections and frustrations during my career, yet I've always made it a point to have enough financial resources to maintain a certain amount of security in my lifestyle…even if I had to temporarily put my artistic pursuits on a back burner in order to accomplish it.

I guess that's why, despite my many successes, I've always been somewhat of an outsider in the entertainment industry. I've worked and become friends with people on both the artistic and the business sides of Hollywood, but I never really joined either "team".

For better or worse, I always went my own way.

And that started with my family.

I come from a nice upper middle class Jewish family. We weren't rich. We were "comfortable".

My father, Harry Druxman, was a successful Seattle jeweler. My mother, Florence, was a successful Seattle Jewish American Princess who'd married a man twenty-seven years her senior. Both had been married before, and I had a half-brother (Hersh) on my father's side, with a son (Pat) a year younger than me. Five years after I was born, I would also get a younger brother, Barry.

Like most of us who lean toward the artistic, I was filled with insecurities. I was born in February of 1941, so during my early years, I was always hearing the grown-ups talk about "the war" and bad people, like Germans and Japs, who wanted to hurt us. I had nightmares about these people, and it didn't really help to soothe my young fears when after I would hear thunder and see lightning, my father would announce, "Oh, that's the war."

Of course, when my mother told me that I'd been a breech birth, and that if there had been complications during my delivery, the doctors would have sacrificed me to save her, that didn't calm my fears either.

My mother was always telling me scary things. Once, she told me that, if I ever saw a strange toy lying in our backyard, I should not touch it, because it could be a bomb sent across the ocean via balloon by the Japanese to kill us.

Do you wonder why I never really enjoyed going outside to play?

If it wasn't the Japanese Empire out to get me, then it was this neighbor girl who lived two doors up the street from us.

For the first eleven years of my life, we lived at 1239 23rd East (actually, at that time, it was called 23rd *North*). After that, we moved up the street into a house that my father had had built, 1200 23rd East, which was the family home until my parents passed away in the last half of the 1960s.

As I would discover many years later, my father was, inadvertently, the cause of the problem I had with the neighbor girl, Frankie, who was a year or two older and was always picking on me. Apparently, Dad had purchased our home at 1239 from her grandmother.

I was six or seven years old when, one day, Frankie, for no apparent reason, picked up a brick and threw it at me, hitting me in the head. I had one hell of a lump on my forehead, but I was okay. I ran home crying. My parents were furious. They got on the phone to Frankie's folks and, as I recall, I don't think I ever saw her again.

I'm sure they didn't kill her, but….

Actually, that family was lucky that Dad didn't storm over there and start throwing punches. He had a quick temper and was known to do that. There were many men, much taller than his 5 foot, 8 inches, who wound up on their backs seeing stars…and not the kind you see in movies.

He even punched out my mother's psychiatrist, but that story is probably best left untold.

Now, let's jump ahead thirty years. I'm planning to visit family in Seattle with my six-year-old son, David, and I decide that, while we're there, I would like to show him the house at 1239, which I haven't been inside since I was eleven. I write to the current owners, and they tell me to "absolutely come ahead. We would love to know the history of the house."

As you might expect, the house was much smaller than I remembered, and it was rather disheartening to see some of the radical changes that had been made to it over the years. Nevertheless, I learned something from that visit that made Frankie's actions toward me thirty years earlier "understandable".

The current owners of the house, a nice couple and new parents, were both attorneys. They had done a title check on the property, going back to when the house was first built, and according to those records, my father had purchased the house from Frankie's grandmother for a lot less money than she had originally paid for it.

That didn't surprise me. Dad always paid cash for everything (even his houses), and he always drove a hard bargain.

I assume that Frankie had overheard her parents and her grandmother talking about "that damn Harry Druxman," and how "he'd cheated her out of her house," so I'm sure she felt justified in avenging her Grandma (who always seemed to be scowling) on me. Whether the fact that we were the only Jews on the block contributed to the state of affairs, I will never really know.

From the late 1940s into the early 1960s, our family had a summer home in Soap Lake, Washington, but before that, we had a vacation home closer to Seattle on Lake Lucerne. It had a house, a dock, rowboats; a charming, scenic peaceful place.

On one particular day, my brother, Hersh, was in his swim trunks, and he was moving our rowboat that was sitting partially on the beach, so that it could be tied to the dock. As he pushed the boat all the way into the water, I saw that a large catfish was under it and that she had laid her eggs. Those eggs had hatched and what appeared to be hundreds of baby catfish were swimming about in the shallow water.

Without realizing it, my brother was stepping on those babies, crushing them into the sand.

He was killing the baby fish!

I was probably four years old, maybe younger, when I saw that, but that disturbing image has stuck in my mind for well over sixty years.

You shrinks who are reading this may interpret that as you like.

I was never a lonely kid, but I was a loner. I much preferred my own company, and its accompanying fantasies, rather than doing the things that "normal" kids do. While other children were outside playing football or baseball or whatever, I stayed in my room, preparing for my emergence into greatness.

This was not a great loss for football, baseball or any other sport. I have never been much of a competitor and, when forced to partake in athletic competitions in school or when my parents insisted, I was always the last one chosen for a team.

I know that some of you will consider this to be un-American, but I don't watch the Super Bowl, the World Series or the Olympics. When the morning paper arrives, I toss the "Sports" section and go immediately to "Arts and Entertainment".

Does it surprise you that my stepsons speculated if I was gay?

When I was young, I drew my own comic books, until it dawned on me that I had absolutely no talent for drawing. My straight lines were crooked, even with a ruler.

I also had a Jerry Mahoney doll, and tried my hand at ventriloquism. I wasn't good at that either, but I did win five dollars in a school talent contest once.

Like many boys, I also had a go at being a magician. Saturdays, after seeing a movie, I would frequent Gene Foley's Magic Shop, located across the street from the Palomar Theater on Third Avenue, and I always wound up buying a new trick or two. With my cousin, Lewis, as my assistant, I put on shows for fund-raising carnivals at various elementary schools.

My favorite trick was the one where you have six cards, take away five of them, and still have six left. That illusion had a marvelous patter, and I was quite good delivering it.

No, I'm not going to tell you how the trick was done.

Movies, however, were my passion. Every Saturday after I was allowed to take the bus by myself, I would be in downtown Seattle, being transported to other times and places, while sitting in the Orpheum, Music Hall, Coliseum, Liberty, Roosevelt, Blue Mouse, Music Box or one of the other magnificent Seattle movie houses that no longer exist.

How did I learn screenplay structure and how to write dialogue? Not from books or going to a cinema school. Although I didn't realize it was happening at the time, I learned it from watching movies.

Even my movie-going habits made me an outsider. Sure, I enjoyed films like *The Beast from 20,000 Fathoms*, *Them!*, *The Creature from the Black Lagoon* and *House of Wax*, but when kids my age were fawning over Elvis Presley, Pat Boone and Connie Francis movies, my favorite stars were Edward G. Robinson, James Cagney, George Raft, Randolph Scott, John Wayne, Broderick Crawford and, especially, Humphrey Bogart.

Everybody knows where they were when they heard that JFK was shot or on 9/11. Well, I know exactly where I was when I heard that Humphrey Bogart had died.

I was sitting in Drama Class at Garfield High School when my friend, Gene Rice, came in and made the announcement. I didn't believe him, and I was so upset that I left the classroom, ran down to the school's pay phone and called the local paper to confirm it.

That's right! I was really a weird kid.

When I was thirteen years old, I started collecting 8x10 movie stills and press books.[1] One wall in my bedroom had a large corkboard on it, and it was always filled with a display of movie stills and advertising art that would be changed on a regular basis. One collage might feature Humphrey Bogart or James Dean (I had a set of color stills from all three of his movies), while others might be devoted to Westerns, musicals or gangster movies.

To obtain all this material, I would not only haunt the major studio's film exchanges on Seattle's "Film Row" monthly, but every week or two, I would make the rounds of the downtown movie theaters. My spiel was the same everywhere I went: "Do you have any extra movie stills or press books that you can spare?"

The managers of these exchanges and theaters liked me. Why shouldn't they? I was a nice, polite clean-cut kid. I seldom went away empty handed.

Besides, back in the 1950s, once a film had played out, theaters and exchanges had no use for those stills or press books. Anything they didn't give to me would probably wind up in the trash.

If only they knew then what we know now. Today, that vintage promotional material sells to collectors for big bucks.

Once again, let's jump ahead a few years to the 1970s.

I still had my still collection and continued to add to it. These photos were invaluable in illustrating the movie-oriented books I wrote (e.g. *Basil Rathbone: His Life and His Films, Make It Again, Sam: A Survey of Movie Remakes*, etc.). After I left Seattle, most of the 8x10 photos would be purchased at various bookstores that populated Hollywood Boulevard back then.

One of these bookstores charged a substantial price for stills they had in their inventory, particularly the linen-backed ones from *The Maltese Falcon, The Adventures of Robin Hood* and other vintage films made by Warner Brothers. The owners were also rather nasty.

---

1. Press books were promotional manuals that were sent by the movie studios to theaters that were playing their films. They were filled with canned publicity stories, photos, marketing ideas and pictures of print ads to aid the individual theater managers in selling the movie in their local area. Press books pretty much disappeared from the scene in the early 1980s when the promotion of motion pictures began being handled almost exclusively on a national level.

Around that same time, people in the Warner Brothers publicity department with whom I had worked regularly[2] allowed me access to their library of production stills, so that I could find further illustrations for my books.

I found little in the library that was useful, and when I asked the librarian why there were no books of stills from the classic Warner films of the 1930s and 1940s, he said, "They were stolen one night a few years ago."

I thought about that for a moment, then asked: "Were these stills linen-backed?"

"Yes."

"How would you like to get them back?"

The next day, a couple of people from Warner Brothers walked into that bookstore and bought some of their stolen stills to use as evidence. A few days after that, the cops came into the store with a subpoena and took charge of whatever was left of the Warner Brothers' property. The bookstore owners may not have removed the stills from the studio themselves, but they were certainly guilty of receiving stolen goods.

I'm not sure, but I don't think that anybody went to jail. As I recall, the bookstore agreed not to contest the studio's claim and that ended the matter.

The folks at Warner Brothers were grateful for my helping them get their property back. For the next several years, they were always cooperative when I needed some special favor with regard to a client or one of my books.

I know. Some of you are thinking, *"Druxman's a rat! A stoolie!"*

If this were a James Cagney or Edward G, Robinson gangster movie, I'd have wound up in the East River with a canary in my mouth.

But, doesn't the Bible say something about not stealing?

Nick Furfaro was a nice (and patient) man I met during my early years of collecting. He was the manager of Seattle's magnificent Orpheum Theater, and every week he would give me all his press books and stills from the previous week's picture. The doorman, a tall, quite elderly, gent named "Bill," got to know me and, eventually, he started letting me into the theater free.

Nick (and Bill) would later be transferred over to the Blue Mouse Theater on Fifth Avenue, which was two doors up the street from my

---

2. Producer Philip D'antoni (*Bullitt*) and director Hy Averback (*I Love You, Alice B. Toklas*) were among my publicity clients who worked at the studio.

father's jewelry store. He and my folks would become good friends and, indeed, Nick and I would remain friends for many years. Still later, when I was in my last year of college, Nick would quit the theater business and take over the Magic Inn, one of Seattle's better nightclubs.

I recall seeing singer Jimmie Rogers there and, that same night, I met and shared a table with a seemingly quite angry African-American comedian who was in town to appear at a civil rights benefit. After he'd chatted with Nick, my date and myself for a while, Nick talked him into doing fifteen minutes for the club audience.

I'd never heard of the guy before that night, but he was quite good. "Anger," as I would learn in years to come, is a plus for many comedians. It makes them funnier.

After the show, I complimented this fellow on his performance and said "goodnight." A few months passed, and I read that he'd been signed to star in a new television series with actor Robert Culp. It was called *I Spy*.

But, except for seeing him on stage in Las Vegas many years later, I never crossed paths with Bill Cosby again.

There's one other story involving my friend, Nick, which I want to share with you.

In the early 1990s, I was back visiting relatives in Seattle and, since I hadn't seen Nick in years, I decided to look him up. Turns out, he was running a strip club in the north end of the city, and he invited me to stop by.

Fran, my girl friend at the time, was traveling with me, so when we got to the club, I suggested that she wait in the car and I would go inside and fetch Nick.

He may have gotten older, but he had not changed. He was still the same, upbeat, friendly guy that I remembered.

As we chatted in the parking lot by my car, a State Patrol vehicle pulled into the lot and drove over to us. A sour-faced officer got out and demanded, "Let me see your I.D.s."

Perusing our driver's licenses, the cop looked at Fran and me, with suspicion, and said, *"California, huh?"*

Whereupon Fran came forth with, *"Yes, he's pimping me, officer."*

I'm glad that cop had a sense of humor.

2

The Employee

MY FOLKS WERE SMART.

Although they were financially comfortable and gave me a small weekly allowance, they insisted that, when I was old enough, I get a part-time job if I wanted to go to the movies, buy books, records and other non-essentials.

When I got into college and realized that, if I were going to descend on Hollywood after graduation I would need a "grub stake," the money I earned and usually spent on "fun stuff" went directly into a savings account.

During the summers in Soap Lake, when I was nine or ten, I would hang around the *Soap Lake Reporter*, the local weekly newspaper office, watching editor Sid Jackson and his staff of two set type and print the paper, which I would then walk around town selling for ten cents each, of which I would retain a three cent commission.

I guess that, between Jackson and our colorful old gardener in Soap Lake, "the Storyman," who fascinated me with his endless tales of Jesse James and Billy the Kid, I was given my first push down the road to ruin.

Correction!

The road to *me* becoming a storyteller.

In high school, I got a job peddling magazine subscriptions door-to-door. That's excellent training for somebody who wants to get into show business. It teaches you how to deal with rejection.

My job was to make appointments for my supervisor, who would then go in and actually make the sale. I'd get a couple of dollars for every sale he closed, which would net me twenty dollars or so a week; pretty good for a teenager working after school in the 1950s.

The supervisor's name was "Reno," and it fit him perfectly. Tall and balding, he was a real "sharpie," the kind of person that one would expect to find running one of those sucker booths in a traveling carnival. But, when I was fifteen years old, he fascinated me.

One day at school, I was summoned down to the vice principal's office where I was put on the phone with a Seattle police detective. He wanted to know all about Reno and what he was doing, but he wouldn't tell me the reason. Later, my father called the Chief of Police to find out what was going on.

Dad was well connected in Seattle. He knew everybody. Not only had be gone to school with Seattle's police and fire chiefs and controversial Teamsters union leader Dave Beck, but his best friend was a superior court judge and both Seattle's present and future mayors were at my bar mitzvah reception.

According to the police chief, Reno was wanted for questioning on a rape charge. About a week earlier, while I was going through a large apartment building, knocking on doors and setting appointments, he was in one of the first floor apartments, having his way with the lady inside.

I never saw Reno again, nor did I ever learn how his criminal matter was resolved. But, that was the end of my magazine selling career.

My first "real" job was as a busboy at Seattle's exclusive Washington Athletic Club. I was sixteen-years-old, and making a dollar an hour, big bucks for me then.

What can I say?

God did not intend for me to be a busboy.

I hated that job.

I hated the head busboy even worse....and he hated me.

His name was "Tony," a short, stocky fellow in his mid-fifties, who can best be described as "a third road company version of Edward G. Robinson doing *Little Caesar*".

The problem was that I was smarter than Tony. He knew it. I knew it, and I let *him* know it whenever I refused to submit to his bullying tactics.

After about a month, he found an excuse to fire me.

I don't blame him. I would have fired me, too.

Shortly after I left the Athletic Club, I was hired to work in a pawnshop, located on the corner of First and Union in downtown Seattle. The place was owned and operated by Dave and Louis Wolfstone, two brothers who should never have been in business together. When one of them was out of the store, the other one would always *kvetch* to me on how the other was "ruining the business".

Actually, they had what was probably the most successful pawnshop in Seattle.

Lou, incidentally, had previously lived in Los Angeles and, back in the 1930s, his son, Billy Lee Wolfstone, had been a supporting player in the "Our Gang" comedies (*aka:* "The Little Rascals").

Working in a pawnshop is great training for just about anything else you want to do with your life. Not only does it teach you how to sell, both merchandise and yourself, but you also learn how to deal with people, the public. I didn't realize it at the time, but the people skills I picked up in the years that I worked for the Wolfstones would prove to be invaluable to me later when I operated my own public relations business and, especially, when I owned a check cashing operation. After all, in check cashing, you are dealing with the same sort of folks who patronize pawnshops. The difference is that, instead of having a stock of hard goods like jewelry, televisions, power tools and the like, your inventory is cash.

The Wolfstones were good to me. I would work for them, off-and-on, usually during the summer months and the Christmas season, for the rest of my high school and most of my college years. In fact, after I moved on, my younger brother, Barry, took over my job, and he would go on to spend most of his career in the jewelry business.

Aside from helping out in my parents' jewelry store from time-to-time (*Never work for your parents!*), the only other job I had before moving to Los Angeles was with Pope and Talbot as a real estate salesman. This was the only job I could get in Seattle after graduation from the University of Washington while my military draft status was in question.[1]

The good thing about being a real estate salesman is that you're pretty much your own boss. You can work as much or as little as you want, so when I wasn't showing houses or trying to pick up listings, I was producing and directing plays (e.g. *Suddenly Last Summer, The Miracle Worker*) for my own community theatre company, Actor's Theatre.

The bad thing about being a real estate salesman is that it's a commission only business. If you don't make sales or list houses that sell, then you don't make a dime.

---

1. I would, ultimately, be classified as 1-Y (i.e. only called in case of war or National Emergency). Luckily, when the Vietnam War came about less than a year later, I had moved to Los Angeles and the Selective Service had apparently forgotten about me.

Actually, for the few months that I was in the business, I did okay. I sold a house, a couple of empty lots and two of my listings sold.

One of those listings caused a bit of a family problem.

My father's younger brother, Nate Druxman, had once been a well-known fight promoter in the Pacific Northwest, who had even promoted a bout with champ Jack Dempsey, but now he was a real estate broker. The Montlake District of Seattle, located about a mile from our Capital Hill house, was pretty much his "exclusive" territory. Unlike most realtors, he didn't belong to an exchange in which all listings were pooled and, when sold, commissions split, 2/3 to the selling office and 1/3 to the listing office.

Except on rare occasions, our families didn't socialize. My father's brothers didn't really like or trust my mother. She was his second wife and much younger than him. They probably thought she was a gold digger who would take Dad "like Grant took Richmond," which she didn't do. Despite their issues, and there were plenty, she stayed with him for over twenty-five years, the rest of his life.

He may have been different with his own family, but I always found my Uncle Nate to be cold and unfriendly towards me, so it didn't help matters much when, while driving to work one day, I stopped by and listed a house in the Montlake District.

Since Pope and Talbot was located miles away in the north end of Seattle, I knew I wasn't going to be able to work that listing myself, hence I telephoned my uncle and offered to split the listing with him. He wasn't interested. "Just because your name is Druxman," he said, "that doesn't give you any special privileges with me." Then, he hung up.

I told my father about that conversation, and he was totally pissed. He got on the phone and started shouting at his brother. "What kind of asshole are you?" he said. "He's your nephew, for Christ's sake. Work with him."

Uncle Nate never did "work" with me and, except for my father's funeral a few years later, I don't believe I ever saw or spoke to him again.

I might have done well had I stayed in the real estate business, but my dreams were pointing me southward. I quit Pope and Talbot in the fall of 1963 and, shortly thereafter, headed for Los Angeles where I would live for the next forty-five years.

But, I'm getting ahead of myself. Time to back up a bit.

3

The Actor

I WAS GOING TO BE AN ACTOR.

Correction: I was going to be *a movie star*.

I knew that from the time I was four-years old when my mother took me to see *Pinocchio*, and I heard that little wooden guy sing, *"Hi, diddly-dee! An actor's life for me!"*

Actually, I was a "star" the first time I ever stepped onto a stage.

I was in the first grade at Stevens Elementary School on 19th Avenue. Our class was doing a short play for the PTA, *Gingham Lena*.

Gingham Lena was a stuffed toy dog that gets lost, and the little girl who owns him spends most of the play looking for him.

I was Gingham Lena. A classmate, Honey MacArthur, who looked like Shirley Temple, played my owner. My mother made this colorful costume for me to wear, complete with floppy ears and tail.

And, I was absolutely brilliant in the role!

After that, I didn't have much opportunity to go on stage until I was at Garfield High School. I did some roles in plays at Seattle's Cirque Playhouse (i.e. *The Bees and The Flowers, You Can't Take It With You*), *Having Wonderful Time* at the Jewish Community Center and Mr. Joseph Steele-Shaw, Garfield's drama teacher, gave me a small part in a school production of *My Sister Eileen*.

It was Mrs. Patricia Borgstrom, who took over Garfield's drama class my senior year, who gave me the opportunity, once again, to be a "star". She cast me as "Remy Marko," the leading role in the senior play, *A Slight Case of Murder*.

In this Damon Runyon comedy, I was playing a retired bootlegger, a part that one of my idols, Edward G. Robinson, had played in the classic 1938 movie and another idol, Broderick Crawford, had reprised in a

1950s remake. Part of my costume was the vest that my father had copied from Robinson's *Little Caesar*.

Years later, Mrs. Borgstrom confessed to me that she had never directed a play before *A Slight Case of Murder*, and really didn't know what the hell she was doing. But, the production turned out okay. We got every laugh we were supposed to get, and I felt totally comfortable on that stage. Indeed, I was in my element.

I was so "in control" of what was happening that, when another actor was having a problem (i.e. breaking concentration, missing a cue, etc.), I was able to pull them back into the moment without the audience knowing there was an issue.

I've always been grateful to "Mrs. B." for giving me what was the happiest and most shining moment during my otherwise unhappy high school years. Back then; she was one of the few people who believed in my talent and what I wanted to do with my life. Although I would talk to her every few months on the telephone, I only saw her twice more after I left Seattle in 1963.

The first was at my 20th high school reunion in 1979, then, in 2004, I was back in Seattle for my 45th high school reunion, and while I was in town, I gave a talk to a class at the University of Washington Drama Department. Mrs. B. was there, and afterwards we went out for a long, enjoyable lunch.

She was 90 when she passed away in 2010, and I do miss her.

My parents weren't overly excited when I told them that, at the University of Washington, I was going to be a Drama Major. They would have much preferred that I study Law, Medicine or Business.

They also knew that, if they fought my decision, I would stand my ground. For years, I'd endured unceasing mocking from my extended family whenever I talked about wanting to be an actor. An aunt once even suggested that, if I wanted to be an actor, I must be "gay."[1] That remark definitely hurt, but I was immovable.

My father's reaction to my announcement: "Well, it's okay to start there."

My mother, who would have been happy if I majored in Philosophy or French or even Home Economics just so I went to and graduated from college, was more encouraging, but I knew that she was figuring that, at some point in time, I'd outgrow my childhood fantasy.

---

1. In fact, the word she used was much less politically correct.

Actually, under the leadership of Glenn Hughes, the UW was considered to have one of the best university drama departments in the United States. The school had three well-equipped theaters that presented plays twelve months every year, and many successful artists (e.g. Robert Culp, Ann Sothern, Frances Farmer, Lois Smith, Clu Gulager) in the entertainment industry had attended or graduated from it.

It was my senior year before I ever took a course taught by Hughes. He said something about the realities of show business during one class that I've never forgotten:

"You may have to pay your technical people, but you can always find actors who will work for free."

That is *so* true.

The summer before I entered the UW, I not only took a two week trip to Hollywood to check out the lay of the land…*and to inform the town that I'd be there in four years and to get ready for me*…but I also tried out for and was cast in a play in Bellevue, which is located across Lake Washington from Seattle.

The play was the funny and delightful *Visit to a Small Planet*, which had starred Cyril Richard on Broadway, then had been destroyed in the movies when Jerry Lewis took over the leading role. Gale Gordon, one of my future publicity clients, was also in that film.

I really wanted a role in that play, the juvenile romantic lead or the general's aide, an army lieutenant. I gave a good reading and the director liked me, but she was wondering if I might be too young for the parts. So, I lied. I was eighteen years old then, but I told her I was twenty-one. I got the role of the lieutenant, which had some good moments.

My problem was that, having told a big fib, I felt that I had to maintain the charade about my age for the next two months during rehearsals and the play's run. Truthfully, I don't think I fooled the director or anybody in the cast, particularly John Gilbert, who played the Cyril Ritchard role and was a junior in the UW Drama Department, but they all went along with my pretense because, if I do say so myself, I gave a good performance, and that's the bottom line.

Going from being the star of my high school senior play to being a lowly freshman in the UW Drama Department was certainly a come down, but it was also the beginning of an exciting adventure.

I was, in fact, fortunate because in 1959-60, my freshman year, there was a shortage of men in the Drama Department. That meant that newcomers, like me, who under ordinary circumstances might only be cast in bit roles in the Department's stage productions, were given the opportunity to play substantial parts and even leads.

The first week of the Fall Quarter, I was cast in a production of *Tall Story*[2], playing two roles, a college student and an FBI agent. The play was directed by Professor Donal Harrington, the primo donna of the school, who (I was told) had been a stage manager on Broadway before he joined the faculty in 1938.

Tall Story would be the first of seven plays, including *The Happiest Millionaire* and *An Inspector Calls*, that I did back-to-back at the Department's Penthouse Theatre, the first permanent theatre-in-the-round built in the United States.[3] At the Cirque Playhouse, I had worked in the 3/4 round, but never in the full round, which was an interesting experience.

When you are working on a proscenium stage, or even in 3/4 round, an actor feels somewhat "protected," but when you are totally surrounded by the audience you are *out there*. You can't check your fly or scratch your butt without half the crowd seeing it.

That first year in the Drama Department was marvelous training for a young actor. It was like being in repertory theatre. Four or five nights each week, I would perform in whatever play that was on the boards. Afternoons, I would be rehearsing the next play, which would open its six-week run immediately after the current one closed. For a couple of the productions, I was even paid to run the lights.

I would also attend classes throughout the morning and early afternoon hours, the regular ones the university required for all students, plus the courses that would result in a Drama degree: Theatre Speech, Stage Make-Up, Costuming, Set Construction, Stage Lighting and, through the English Department, Shakespeare, which I found to be one of the most interesting and enjoyable courses I took during my entire time at the university.

You'll note that I didn't list Acting. That's because a Drama Major was not allowed to take those classes until his sophomore year.

But, who needed acting lessons? I was on stage almost every night practicing the craft. Is there any better teacher than experience?

---

2. *Tall Story* would later be made into a movie starring Anthony Perkins and Jane Fonda.

3. All of these Penthouse productions would also be presented for two nights at Seattle's Washington Athletic Club, a large financial contributor to the Drama Department, and where I'd once worked briefly as a busboy.

Orson Welles said it, and I'm paraphrasing: "If you want to make movies, you can go to film school for four years, or you can go out and make a movie."

The caveat of that position, which certainly also applies to theatre, is that, if you want to be successful in the "learn by doing" approach, you'd better be sure that experienced people surround you. They can help insure that, as brilliant an artist as you might be; practical matters don't cause you to fall flat onto your face. Indeed, when he made *Citizen Kane*, Orson Welles was wise enough to have some of the best craftsmen in the business working with him.

One of the most valuable pieces of acting advice that I received in my freshman year was given to me during the run of *Miranda*, a British comedy about a mermaid, portrayed by the beautiful Yoland Johnson. Since this was a summer production with not a lot of men taking classes, Professor Robert Gray, who directed, also wound up doing the male lead.

I was cast as the chauffer who becomes smitten with the ladyfish, and there was one moment in the play where I had a reaction that garnered a huge laugh from the audience. Every night, I'd react, and I'd bring down the house, as they say.

But, after the first week or so, I stopped getting that laugh. I'd react, and there was dead silence from the audience. This went on for two or three performances, so I asked Professor Gray, a kindly man, what I was doing wrong.

"You're anticipating the laugh," he said.

He was absolutely right. The next night, I didn't anticipate. I played the moment, and the big laugh was back, as it was for the rest of the show's run.

Unfortunately, I did not get along with Professor Harrington, as well as I did with Professor Gray.

There were no issues when I worked with him in *Tall Story*, but later in the year, he cast me in a production of *The Taming of the Shrew*. Not only had I never performed Shakespeare before, but also I was totally miscast in the role of "Grumio," manservant to "Petruchio" and the lead "clown" in the play.

Instead of helping me to become more comfortable in a part for which I felt totally unsuited, Harrington made me his "whipping boy." He had a reputation for picking one cast member to heap abuse upon in every show he directed, and in this instance, I was it.

He would shout directions at me. I'm not a stupid person, but I honestly didn't understand what he wanted. On one occasion, at the end of the rehearsal when he was giving notes to the entire cast, he looked at me and said, "You stink up the play every time you walk on stage."

I'm sure you can imagine how humiliating that was. Had that happened a few years later, I would have told him to go fuck himself and walked out. But, I was a lowly freshman, and had I done that, he could have made life impossible for me for the next four years.

Playing "Katherine" in that production was my dear friend (and future publicity client), Marian Hailey, who would later do several shows on Broadway, including a revival of *Harvey* with Jimmy Stewart and Helen Hayes, and also play key roles in some films, most notably the Oscar-winning *Lovers and Other Strangers* (1970).

Marian recently admitted to me that perhaps the biggest mistake she ever made was turning down a running role in the classic television soap, *Dark Shadows*. "I wanted to do Shakespeare," she said. "That was a stupid career move."

We did *Shrew*. The audience seemed to respond well to me. I guess I did okay, but I never really felt I belonged in that production. Although, in a recent e-mail, Marian also said to me, "I can remember how very earnest you were in that role to this day."

There is absolutely no acceptable excuse for an actor missing an entrance. It is totally unprofessional. But, I did it once at the Penthouse in a production of a play, *To Have the Honour* by A.A. Milne.

My part was rather small in that show. I was in the opening scene, and then I had one other scene midway through the play. There was nothing for me to do in between.

The dressing rooms at the Penthouse were wired for sound, so you could hear what was happening on stage. I was in the dressing room, chatting with another actor, when the speaker above the door went totally silent. Gary Hagar, who was the leading man in the play, was on stage… all by himself…waiting for my entrance.

"Oh, shit!" I said, as I dashed out the dressing room door, and ran halfway around the circular lobby that surrounded the stage to where I made my entrance.

Gary could definitely hear me coming, and so could the audience. They were certainly smiling when I burst through those curtains onto the stage.

That was probably my most embarrassing moment as an actor. I can assure you that nothing like that ever happened again.

About the same time that we were doing *The Taming of the Shrew* at the Penthouse, I was cast in another Shakespeare production that was being produced as a television special by the university's Radio-TV Department, which shared the same building as the Drama Department and also operated Seattle's only educational television channel.

Rod Whitaker, then working for his Master's Degree at the UW, had adapted and was going to direct a one-hour version of *Hamlet* to be broadcast *live* over the channel. I'm not positive, but I believe that this is the first time a dramatic production, originated at the university, would be broadcast, so it was going to be promoted as a major event.

Rod would later become a respected film scholar, and also, using the pen name "Trevanian," he was a successful novelist. Perhaps his best-known work, *The Eiger Sanction*, was made into a 1975 movie, directed by and starring Clint Eastwood.

John Gilbert, with whom I had appeared in *Visit to a Small Planet* and would, later, become a prominent member of the acting company at the Seattle Repertory Theater, played "Hamlet." Marian Hailey was "Ophelia" and David Seidler, who in 2010 would win an Academy Award for writing *The King's Speech*, was "Claudius."

I was cast as "Osric." In the Laurence Olivier movie version, Peter Cushing played that part and in Kenneth Branagh's more recent filming, Robin Williams assumed the role.

What can I say?

"Osric" is a fop, but he gets to deliver a memorable Shakespearian line: *"A hit, a very palpable hit."*

My parents watched the live broadcast. When I came home that night, they said they enjoyed it, though I suspect my father, who was in his seventies at the time and not the most tolerant person, probably was a bit embarrassed at my playing such an effeminate role...particularly on television.

On the other hand, my aunt certainly had a bit more ammunition to support her claims about my masculinity.

As I recall, there were no flubs in that live broadcast, which is quite remarkable. The show was well received by both the public and the press, and over the years, the station re-broadcast it several times.

I am proud of the fact that I was a part of that special production. I only wish that I had a copy of it. Sadly, when I contacted the university a few years ago to see if I could purchase one, I was told that it no longer existed.

4

The Actor/Director

AT THE START OF MY SOPHOMORE YEAR, everything changed.

The Drama Department had plenty of new men enrolled, mostly juniors, seniors and graduate students.

In my freshman year, I'd been cast in some solid supporting roles, and I'd even been given a co-lead, but now the handwriting was on the wall. Those choice parts were going to be given to the older students.

I was offered a part in a production of Thomas Wolfe's *Look Homeward, Angel*, which was going to be done at the school's Showboat Theatre. The play had a large cast and this was a small role, so I turned it down.

My reasoning at the time was that, after playing so many substantial parts, doing what was, in essence, a large bit, would be a step backward. It would be two months wasted on a thankless role.

I know: *There are no small roles, just small actors.*

I probably made a mistake by refusing the part, because I never did another play at the UW again. Actually, if my memory is correct, I don't think I ever auditioned for another play at the university.

But, something else was going on with me then. After doing seven plays back-to-back, I'd become a bit bored with acting.

Been there. Done that.

I took the Department's acting classes. They taught the Stanislavski Method, and that also bored me.

Why did I have to pretend to be an animal?

Nevertheless, I did the "Method" exercises and, by the way, I chose to be a parrot.

Sometime during that year, I had an epiphany. I realized that, unlike Pinocchio, I wasn't an "actor". I was really more of a "performer," even though I didn't sing or dance. And, I had no interest in becoming a stand-up comedian, yet I could be funny and I possessed a good sense of comedy timing.

Instead, I was developing a strong yen to direct. Unfortunately, one had to be a senior to take directing courses in the Drama Department.

I began looking for directing opportunities outside of the Department, perhaps in community theatre.

It was also during my sophomore year that I changed majors.

I realized that if I ever wanted to get a job outside of the entertainment industry, having been a Drama Major would not look good on a résumé, particularly in Los Angeles where a prospective employer would figure that you were just marking time until you were discovered by the movies.

Perhaps there was also another reason. I am neither gay nor homophobic, but I was getting a little tired of certain relatives, as well as some of my fraternity brothers at ZBT, questioning my sexual preference. Back in the early 1960s, people had not yet come "out of the closet," and the consensus of many students at the UW was that, if you were in the Drama Department, you were probably gay.

I switched to Sociology. I really had no interest in that field, but I had taken an introductory course to satisfy one of the university's social science requirements; I had enjoyed it and, since only seven more courses were required in the field to obtain a Bachelor of Arts degree, I figured "Why not?" I could still take any Drama courses that were of interest, as well as some courses in the UW's Radio-TV Department, and if I weren't doing plays in the Department, I would have time to explore opportunities in Seattle's community theaters.

I don't recall how it came about, but I became involved with the Boards Playhouse, a well-regarded community theatre that operated out of a huge old movie theater in West Seattle. They had a commitment to present a one-act play, something to do with senior health care, for, I believe, a nursing association. Truthfully, I can't remember the name of the play, the name of the association or any of the other specific details about the situation, except that I was offered the opportunity to direct the project.

I'm sure I wasn't their first choice. Their regular directors probably turned down the assignment.

What I *do* remember about the single performance we presented is that, during the first scene, the leading actress forgot her lines, skipped the second scene altogether and jumped into scene three.

Sitting in the back of the auditorium, I was helpless to do anything about this potential disaster, but luckily, I had a couple of more experienced actors on stage with her and they got the show back on track.

That was the problem doing amateur theatre. Sometimes you got good actors and other times you were stuck with "bodies" who could barely recite their lines to fill roles that had to be cast.

Actually, that can happen in professional theatre, too, but, thankfully, not often.

I enjoyed the directing experience and, apparently the people at the Boards Playhouse thought I did a good job, because during the summer between my college sophomore and junior years, they let me direct a production on their main stage.

I was twenty years old and I was going to be a *real* director!

Eat your heart out, Drama Department!

The play was *Blue Denim* by James Leo Herlihy and William Noble. It dealt with teen pregnancy and abortion. Carol Lynley and Warren Berlinger, both of whom I would get to know years later in Hollywood, had done the show on Broadway, then repeated their roles in the 1959 movie version that had also featured Brandon De Wilde in the leading part. Carol, in fact, would do the first staged reading of my one-woman play, (Carole) *Lombard*.

Blue Denim was cast. Rehearsals began and, after the first week or so, it became apparent that the fellow that I had cast in the Brandon De Wilde role was not working out…and I didn't have a suitable replacement.

In amateur theatre, you always have plenty of actresses auditioning for roles, but never enough actors.

The actor I'd cast as the lead's father suggested that I assume the role. He was a tall man, probably in his late thirties or early forties, whose day job was being a pharmacist. He was also gay, which was okay. But, he had "designs" on me, which was *not* okay with me…or with the divorced, slightly older lady with whom I was carrying on a hot affair at the time.

Nevertheless, with his encouragement, I did the stupid thing and let my ego trump my better judgment. I took over the leading role and also continued to direct the play.

Dumb! Dumb! Dumb!

I was twenty years old; directing my first play and now I was also starring in it.

To make matters worse, this fellow also convinced me that it should be billed as "A Michael Druxman Production".

Who the hell did I think I was?
Laurence Olivier or Orson Welles?
Yeah, I guess I did.
Putz!

The production that we presented wasn't a disaster, but it wasn't terrific either. Thankfully, the other actors were good in their roles, and were praised by the newspaper reviewers, who were not impressed with my acting, but they did give me points for my direction.

With the exception of doing an Alfred Hitchcock-like walk-on in my movie, *The Doorway* (2000), I never acted in anything I directed again.

After *Blue Denim* closed its six-week run, The Boards Playhouse went through a management shake-up, and I pretty much stayed away from what was going on there during my junior year at the UW. But, in the spring of 1962, I became active again.

I had fallen in love with Arthur Miller's *Death of a Salesman*; arguably the greatest and most powerful play of the American Theatre. More than anything else, I wanted to direct a production of that classic.

After all, I was now an "experienced" director.

Move over, Elia Kazan![1] I'm coming through!

Is there anything more asinine than the ego of a twenty-one-year-old?

Nevertheless, I was a good salesman, even back then, and I sold the Boards Playhouse, now renamed The Seattle Civic Playhouse, on letting me stage Miller's play…right after they did a production of Sidney Kingsley's *Detective Story*.

The community theatre was having major financial difficulties, and the fact that 1962 was the summer of Seattle's World Fair didn't help matters. Rent on the facility was past due, but the owners of the property agreed to "work" with the theatre for a few months. *Detective Story* had been selected because, aside from being a terrific play, it had a large cast, and in community theatre, large casts draw in large audiences (i.e. friends, relatives).

Detective Story did well for the Seattle Civic Playhouse. I, in fact, even took a small role in the production.

One afternoon during that period, I went down to the fairgrounds and got hired to be an extra in *It Happened at the World's Fair*, the MGM movie that was shooting in Seattle starring Elvis Presley. If you see the picture, not one of Elvis' best, you should be able to spot me in a scene with Elvis and a young Kurt Russell.

---

1. Kazan directed the original Broadway production of *Death of a Salesman*.

While *Detective Story* was playing its successful run, I cast and began rehearsing *Death of a Salesman*.

Like Hamlet or King Lear, Willy Loman is a role that most good actors would kill to be cast in, and I knew that without a fine actor in that part, there would be no sense in going ahead with the production. I approached Fred Bornhoeft, a graduate student and the finest actor in the UW Drama Department. Several years my senior, Fred's acting style reminded me of Paul Muni, who had starred in the London production of *Death of a Salesman*.

With Fred on board, I was able to enlist several more of Seattle's better players for the production. They included Drama Department student Brennan O'Connor as "Linda" and, my friend, William "Bill" Turner, who would later be my "Big Daddy" in *Cat on a Hot Tin Roof*, as "Charley". I also had a good "Biff," "Bernard" and "Howard," but for a couple of the other key roles, I was forced to employ "bodies".

Such is the world of amateur theatre.

No question that I was really way over my head trying to take on such a complex play as *Death of a Salesman* back then, yet with Fred's friendship and help, we were able to pull off a pretty decent production. Called "a moderate success" by one of the newspaper critics, the staging was one of the biggest grossers that the theater ever had, but even those box-office receipts were not strong enough to save the Seattle Civic Playhouse. *Death of a Salesman* would be its final production.

To the best of my knowledge, Fred Bornhoeft never pursued a professional acting career, which is a shame. His was an amazing talent, and I sincerely believe that he could have become a major character star in both the Broadway theatre and motion pictures.

With the Seattle Civic Playhouse gone and me about to begin my final year at the UW, I started looking around for other directing opportunities. I found one at the Belfry Playhouse, headquartered in a former church and located in Bellevue, the Seattle suburb where I'd appeared in *Visit to a Small Planet* a few years earlier.

The Belfry had been formed and, I assume, initially financed by a woman named Dorothy Saunders, a one-time, long retired professional stage actress, who was then well into her seventies. She had planned a season of vintage melodramas, like *Love Rides the Rails*, that were so ancient that they creaked. She asked me to direct one of these productions, but I knew that there would be no audience interest in them, so I suggested a few more recent plays as alternatives, none of which she liked.

Perusing a play catalog while I was on the phone with her, I came across *Laura*, a stage version of Vera Caspary's famous mystery novel, which been turned into the classic 1944 movie starring Gene Tierney, Dana Andrews, Clifton Webb and Vincent Price. I had never read the stage play, but since I loved the film, I suggested it and, without hesitation, Dorothy agreed.

Shortly thereafter, I actually read the play and was immediately stricken with an acute case of "buyer's remorse". It was not anywhere as good as the movie or what I'd expected. Produced in 1947, it had, in fact, flopped on Broadway.

However, being a man of my word, I proceeded with the production, which despite the rather dreary script, turned out all right and made money for the theater.

Laura is where I met Ed Siemens, who would become a lifelong friend, and it's also where I met Terry, who would become my first wife and the mother of my son, David. She came in and auditioned for the title role, but I didn't cast her. Instead, I made her my assistant director.

Dorothy Saunders may have founded the Belfry Playhouse, but other, younger people in the group were actually running the operation, and they were not happy with Dorothy's choices of non-commercial plays. Neither was I, so after the success of my production of *Laura*, I sold these young "upstarts" on the idea of doing a play by perhaps the most commercial playwright of that day, Tennessee Williams. And, the play that we chose to do was *Cat on a Hot Tin Roof*.

Before *Cat* went onto the boards, The Belfry had scheduled a production of *The Grass is Greener*, a British romantic comedy by Hugh and Margaret Williams that had been turned into a 1960 movie with Cary Grant, Deborah Kerr and Robert Mitchum. It dealt with a happily married, currently bored, British noblewoman, who has an affair with an American millionaire. Grant and Kerr played the married couple and Mitchum was the likeable other man.

In the Belfry production, Terry was cast as the noblewoman. Although at twenty-two, I was too young for the role, I was asked to play the Robert Mitchum part. I had never played a romantic part before, so I jumped at the opportunity. I even grew a mustache to help correct the age situation, but that didn't really help. Somebody quipped that, instead of making me appear older, the mustache made me look like "an Italian immigrant".

The Belfry production of *The Grass is Greener* was significant in my life for two reasons. Not only was this to be the last time I would ever act on stage, but it also marked the start of my romantic relationship with Terry, who was over eight years older than me, married (unhappily) and with three children. Indeed, our relationship mirrored what was happening on stage, and it wouldn't be long before the people at the Belfry knew it.

Looking back, I am certainly not proud of my part in breaking up a marriage. Because of my selfish immaturity, I hurt a lot of people, and I am truly sorry for that.

But, this book is not meant to be about my romantic life. It's supposed to be about my adventures in show business, so we'll move on.

As a director, I really came into my own with *Cat on a Hot Tin Roof*. For the first time, I felt "secure" in the director's chair. I understood Williams' play backwards and forwards, and I was able to convey my vision to a talented and receptive cast.

Terry played "Maggie," and she was terrific; certainly one of the most talented actresses with whom I've ever worked. I've always felt that, had she taken that road, Terry could have had a successful career as a professional actress.

Others in the cast were my friend, Bill Turner, as "Big Daddy" and Ann Gray, also a Garfield High School alumnus, as "Mae". Ann and I had appeared together in the Jewish Community Center production of *Having Wonderful Time*, she was my assistant on *Blue Denim* and, despite my previous claim that this book is not about my romantic life, I am compelled to say a few words about her.

Ann Gray was the most beautiful girl at Garfield High. If she'd ever given me a serious tumble, I would have probably married her in a minute, but she didn't. We dated. We were (and still are) good "buddies," yet despite my efforts, nothing romantic ever happened between us.

On one occasion during my college years, I got tickets for a new play starring Rod Steiger that was trying out at Seattle's Moore Theatre. I figured that I'd woo Ann with a date that she'd never forget, so before the show I took her to Pancho's, one of Seattle's finest restaurants…and owned by my uncle.

The manager of Pancho's had been tipped off that we were coming. When Ann and I got there, we were treated like movie stars: "Oh, Mr. Druxman, so nice to see you again…."

She was certainly impressed and the rest of the evening went well, but the "spark" just wasn't there.

Ann, who has been happily married for years and now lives in Portland, Oregon, is the one who got away.

Then again, had Ann and I gotten together, we probably would have killed each other. Politically, we are on totally different ends of the spectrum. Truly, how James Carville and Mary Matalin are able to live under the same roof continually baffles me.

Cat on a Hot Tin Roof was a bittersweet success for me. Artistically, everything worked. The audience response was all I could have asked for, and the production did extremely well financially.

However, during one performance, there was one minor hiccup.

I had decided to use Williams' *original* third act, as opposed to the one that was presented on Broadway. My reasoning was both artistic and pragmatic. On the one hand, I felt that the more downbeat ending in the original was truer to the material that had come before it. I also knew that Bill Turner, who was well into his sixties, had trouble learning lines. Since "Big Daddy" did not appear on-stage in the original third act, I figured that that would make Bill's job easier.

"Big Daddy" may not have come on-stage during the third act, but he did have to scream in pain a couple of times off-stage. On this particular night, I was standing in the back of the auditorium, pleased with a performance that was going well.

But, when it came time for "Big Daddy" to scream, there was no scream. Terry, Ann Gray and the other actors stood there for a moment, then started ad-libbing, praying for that off-stage wail that motivated the remainder of the scene.

Nothing. Dead silence.

Springing into action, I bolted out the back door of the auditorium, sprinted down to the stage door, opened it, stuck my head inside and screamed. The play continued.

As it turned out, Bill had been sitting off-stage, following the play in his script, waiting for his cue to scream. Unfortunately, his thumb had been sitting over the part of the script that contained his cue.

So, I guess the guilty party was Big Daddy's big thumb!

Despite the fact that *Cat* had turned out well, this had been a problem production from the start.

Back in the early 1960s, Bellevue was a small conservative town, and Tennessee Williams was a controversial playwright who not only utilized dirty words in his plays, like "bastard" and "ass," but also dealt with controversial subject matter, such as homosexuality, which was a key theme in *Cat*. Interestingly, the 1958 movie version of *Cat* with Elizabeth Taylor and Paul Newman totally eliminated the homosexual angle from the screenplay, but director Richard Brooks and MGM had much more latitude with their script than did the Belfry Playhouse with the original play.

After they had announced *Cat* as their next production and we were well into rehearsal, some members of the Board of Directors actually read the play and were shocked…SHOCKED…at some of vile language that, they thought, would offend the community. They threatened that, if changes in the script were not made, the production would not proceed.

"Well," I suggested, "we could change 'ass' to 'tush,' and 'bastard' to 'momzer'. Half the audience wouldn't know what we were saying then, so that would be okay."

The Board didn't appreciate my humor. After some spirited negotiations that involved a lot of shouted words worse than those we were asked to eliminate, a few minor changes were made and the show went on.

Actually, I had the Board and the theater over a barrel. The cast of *Cat* was backing me, and if I'd walked, they would have followed, which meant that the Belfry stage would be dark for well over a month, since there was no other play on their schedule.

Though I'd won the censorship battle and given them a show that played to full houses every night, hard feelings remained between the Board and me. I don't think that either one of us wanted to work with the other again.

That was fine with me, because I had other plans.

5

The Producer/Director

THEATRE IN SEATTLE DURING THE 1950S and early 1960s was a mixed bag. The national companies of Broadway hits would occasionally pass through the city, playing anywhere from two days to a couple of weeks at either the Orpheum or Moore Theaters in the downtown area.

Even when I was a young teenager, whenever I could afford it, I would take in one of these road companies. At the Orpheum, I recall seeing *My Fair Lady* with Michael Evans, *The Music Man* with Forrest Tucker and Joan Weldon, *Bye, Bye Birdie* with Bill Hayes and Elaine Dunn, *The Caine Mutiny Court-Martial* with Paul Douglas, Wendell Corey and Steve Brodie and *The Andersonville Trial* with Brian Donlevy; at the Moore, *Damn Yankees* with burlesque legend Bobby Clark, *The Desperate Hours* with William Gargan, Nancy Colman and Richard Jaeckel, Rod Steiger in *A Short Happy Life*, *Come Blow Your Horn* with Hal March, the great Morris Carnovsky and Warren Berlinger ; and, in a theater somewhere on the World's Fair grounds, the road company of *Camelot* with Kathryn Grayson (a future publicity client), Louis Hayward and Arthur Treacher.

Seeing these professional productions made me even more determined to become a part of the show business world.

One other play that I saw at the Moore was a light risqué comedy, *Pajama Tops*, starring *Playboy* magazine favorite June Wilkinson and John Agar (*Fort Apache, Tarantula!*), both of whom I would get to know years later in Hollywood. Ms. Wilkinson, in fact, had a major role in *Keaton's Cop* (1990), my first feature film writing credit and a movie that we would both like to forget. June and I have maintained a friendship over the years. She is a delightful, charming and talented lady.

Beyond the sporadic professional productions that came to Seattle, the University of Washington gave local theatre goers the classics (e.g.

Shakespeare, Chekhov), as well as older comedies (George Bernard Shaw, Noel Coward) and dramas (Eugene O'Neill, J.B. Priestley). Community theatres usually did more current comedies and light dramas, and the semi-professional Cirque Playhouse would bring in a "name" actor to star with local players in a popular comedy or drama *of their choosing*. Over the years at the Cirque, I saw Jane Darwell in *Arsenic and Old Lace*, John Carradine in *The Winslow Boy*, Sterling Holloway in *The Seven Year Itch*, Rita Moreno in *Champagne Complex*, Mercedes McCambridge in *The Time of the Cuckoo*, Edward Everett Horton in *The White Sheep of the Family*, Reginald Gardiner in *Visit to a Small Planet* and Stuart Erwin in *Tunnel of Love*, among others.

What Seattle *wasn't* getting were the newer edgy Broadway dramas; plays that community theaters figured might offend their audiences and thus prove to be non-commercial. That's why their seasons were filled mostly with light comedies. They were safer.

My idea was to change all that. The success of *Cat on a Hot Tin Roof* was proof that audiences wanted to see good dramas, controversial or not.

Having an entrepreneurial spirit, I decided to start my own theatrical company. It was my contention that the problem with community theaters was that they were run by boards of directors who practiced "group think" in making artistic decisions. Some community theaters even had "casting committees" that voted on who should get what role in a particular play, taking that decision away from the director.

My company, Actors' Theatre, would be totally different. It would be financed by the actors themselves, but would be run as a benevolent dictatorship. There would be no board making decisions. One person would do the play selection, casting and direct the entire season of plays. *Me!*

I had worked well with the cast of *Cat*. Most of them, some of whom were old enough to be my parents, bolted the Belfry Playhouse and followed this twenty-two-year-old upstart.

Subsequently, we held an open meeting at a downtown hotel, and even more people joined us. Each member of the group was required to invest a minimum of twenty-five dollars in the company, all of which went toward production costs. At the end of each production, the box-office receipts would be split among the contributors. Nobody expected to get all their money back from these shows, let alone make a profit, but the individual investments were so small that nobody really cared. We were "artists," and we were going to do theatre in Seattle that hadn't been done before.

Since *Cat on a Hot Tin Roof* had been so successful, I decided that for Actors' Theatre's premiere production we should do an even more controversial Tennessee Williams play, *Suddenly Last Summer*, which not only dealt with homosexuality, but also cannibalism. A 1959 movie version had starred Elizabeth Taylor, Katharine Hepburn and Montgomery Clift.

Suddenly Last Summer was a long one-act play, not enough for a full evening's entertainment. So, I chose to pair it with a shorter play by Williams, *Twenty-Seven Wagons Full of Cotton*, which had served as the basis for *Baby Doll*, the 1956 film starring Carroll Baker, Karl Malden and Eli Wallach that had run into major censorship problems when it was first released.

Actually, the play I really wanted to kick off Actors' Theatre with was Edward Albee's *Who's Afraid of Virginia Woolf?* I figured if that didn't shock the hell out of 1963 Seattle theatergoers, nothing would. Unfortunately, amateur rights to that play were not yet available.[1]

The casts of the two plays were excellent. Terry took on the Elizabeth Taylor role in *Suddenly Last Summer*, Gene Marshall stood in for Montgomery Clift and Marian Hopkins delivered a deliciously evil rendition of the part played by Katharine Hepburn. For *Twenty-Seven Wagons Full of Cotton*, Ed Siemens' wife, Sydney, did the Carroll Baker role, Bill Turner was in the Karl Malden part, and my good friend from high school, Gene Rice, who had also been in my productions of *Blue Denim*, *Laura* and *Cat on a Hot Tin Roof*, did the Eli Wallach role,

We rehearsed in cast members' living rooms and basements, and then booked the Woman's Century Club Theatre, located just off Broadway at Harvard and Roy Streets, for a two night run. That was all the rent we could afford.

I honestly don't know where it came from, but I've always had a natural knack for promotion and getting publicity. When I was in high school, my father decided to come out of retirement and go back into the jewelry business, and I devised a successful advertising campaign for his store opening, centered around the slogan, "Harry Is Back!".

I have no formal training in the field, but my sixth sense in this area would serve me well a few years later in Hollywood when I started and operated my successful public relations business.

---

1. Shortly after arriving in Los Angeles later that year, I caught the national company of *Who's Afraid of Virginia Woolf?* starring Nancy Kelly, Shepperd Strudwick and Ken Kercheval, who I would get to know better many years later when he and my client, Steve Kanaly, did the *Dallas* television series.

Those instincts also helped with Actors' Theatre. Like with the plays I'd directed previously, I had no problem writing letters or picking up the phone to pitch the newspapers and other local media about our "revolutionary" new project in Seattle theatre. Indeed, Seattle was well informed that Actors' Theatre had arrived.

Suddenly Last Summer/Twenty-Seven Wagons Full of Cotton was well regarded by the audience. Everybody involved considered it to be a winning production, even though the box-office receipts fell short of our investment.

But, we weren't in this to make money. The actors and I wanted to do good theatre. It was decided that for the 1963-64 season, we would do three plays: *The Miracle Worker* by William Gibson, Tennessee Williams' *Sweet Bird of Youth* and *The Bad Seed* by Maxwell Anderson. A brochure was printed and sent to groups that planned theatre parties.

At that point in my life, I was too inexperienced and idealistic to recognize that the business model I'd set up for Actors' Theatre contained two fatal flaws.

First, by dividing up the box-office receipts at the close of every production, Actors' Theatre was left "broke," and was forced to start raising money from scratch for the next show. Were I to do something like this today, I would set it up so that only *a percentage* of the box-office tally would be paid to the investors *at the end of a season*. That way, Actors' Theatre would maintain some working capital to continue.

Second, and certainly most important, productions needed more than just two performances. Aside from the fact that the actors and other folks involved rehearsed and worked for many weeks in order to mount a show and deserved the opportunity to present it for a longer run, the best way to sell a play, a movie or whatever is via "word of mouth". Yes, our productions were well publicized and even advertised in the newspapers, but with them playing only one weekend, reviewers didn't bother attending and by the time that audiences told their friends about it, we had already closed.

If this experiment was going to survive, Actors' Theatre needed to find a more affordable venue where we could mount a longer run.

In the meantime, we were back at the Woman's Century Club Theatre for *The Miracle Worker*.

Once again, I cast Terry in the leading role. She played "Annie Sullivan," and a gifted young lady, Lyn Shela, was "Helen Keller." As those of you who are familiar with this modern classic know, there is a major physical altercation in the second act in which Annie "teaches" Helen to eat properly. Indeed, it's a knockdown, drag out fight. Unlike in the movie version with Anne Bancroft and Patty Duke, these two dedicated actresses did not pull any punches for this scene. They were terrific, and it is a miracle that one of them didn't wind up with a shiner.

The Miracle Worker would be the last production that I would direct for Actors' Theatre, and also the final play I would do in Seattle.

While we were in rehearsals for the play, my draft status had been determined and, since I was not going to have to join the military, I decided that I was going to follow my dream and go to Hollywood.

I turned Actors' Theatre over to Ed Siemens, who would only produce one other play (*Sweet Bird of Youth*). Then a few days after Terry threw me a festive going away party, I got into my car and headed south.

An incredible new adventure in my life was about to begin.

6

Limbo

"The only people who should try to 'make it' in Hollywood are the young.
  Because the young are stupid!
  They cannot conceive of the possibility that they can fail, and a person needs to possess that kind of stupidity in order to face and, hopefully, overcome the tremendous obstacles that one runs up against in the motion picture business."

— Jack Lemmon

ONE OF THE DEFINITIONS OF "LIMBO" found in the dictionary is "a state of uncertainty". And, that's pretty much the state I was in during my first two or three years or so in Los Angeles.

I arrived in town the first week of November 1963, with no show business connections whatsoever. The only people I knew in the city were a couple of actor friends who had moved from Seattle a year or two earlier and were not really active in the business, plus a good friend of my father's, Jack Niaman and his wife, Ida, who didn't know anybody in show business, but who invited me to their Beverly Hills home every Sunday for dinner.

My dad was also old friends with Dr, Nathan Rickles, a respected Beverly Hills psychiatrist, who was then married to actress Lynn Bari. He invited me to his home one afternoon, but beyond some basic advice, there was nothing he could do for me.

Sadly, the one person who *could* have given me a major boost into the motion picture business had retired from the industry two or three years earlier and moved back to his hometown of Cincinnati. He was Fred

Ziv, a second cousin and a television pioneer. His company, Ziv Television, produced such classic syndicated series as *Highway Patrol*, *Sea Hunt* and *The Cisco Kid*. I would not actually meet him, and then only briefly, until I visited Cincinnati, along with Barbara Eden, George Kennedy and my publicity client, Bridget Hanley, for a movie premiere in 1984.

The producers of *Chattanooga Choo Choo*, the totally forgettable picture we were in Cincinnati to promote, put us Hollywood folk up at one the city's oldest and finest hotels, a place where Winston Churchill had once stayed. In fact, Barbara, who I'd known a long time, as she was once married to my friend and client, actor Michael Ansara, was staying in Churchill's old room and, on one occasion, she invited Bridget and me into her bathroom to view the john on which the great man had once sat.

What can I say? It was…a john.

Without any real show business contacts in Hollywood, my game plan was simple. I would find a regular job, and then in my off-hours, I would explore the town; look for opportunities.

I got my first job about three weeks after I'd arrived in town. It was a "management training" position in the sporting goods department of Fedco, a "big box store" for Government employees, located deep in the San Fernando Valley, quite a jaunt from my single apartment in West Hollywood.

The job lasted one day.

That day was November 22, 1963.

Like just about everybody else that day, I walked around in a daze. I spent more time in the television department watching news about President John F. Kennedy's assassination than I did in sporting goods.

The following morning when I left for work, I discovered that the brakes on my car had gone out, so I had to leave it in the repair shop for that day. When I phoned the manager at Fedco, he told me not to bother coming back. Since I had no real knowledge or interest in sporting goods and, frankly, didn't relish that long drive every day on unfamiliar Los Angeles freeways that, at that time, somewhat intimidated me, I didn't give him an argument.

My next job was as an insurance investigator for Retail Credit Company (now Equifax), and I worked there for about a year and a half.

For about three months while I was employed there, I lived in a single apartment on Normandie Avenue, just north of Wilshire Boulevard. That location was much closer to my work than the apartment in West Hollywood, but what was really memorable about it was that I had a rather "infamous" neighbor.

She was Barbara Payton, a former "blonde bombshell" movie actress who had co-starred in movies with Gary Cooper (*Dallas*), James Cagney (*Kiss Tomorrow Goodbye*) and Gregory Peck (*Only the Valiant*). Her career had gone into the dumpster in the early 1950s when she became the center of a public and violent romantic triangle with actors Franchot Tone and Tom Neal. Later, she would be arrested on prostitution charges.

My friend, Michael Ansara, who played a key role in *Only the Valiant*, recalled to me that "Barbara always seemed to be in Gregory Peck's dressing room…and the door was closed."

I never got to know the, by then, grossly overweight and puffy-faced Ms. Payton. She had a poolside apartment and there always seemed to be male company inside. Yet, her story did intrigue me and, years later, I even researched and tried to sell a book about her and her volatile relationship with Tone and Neal, but major publishers were not interested. They felt that nobody in the average reading public would remember those actors whose torrid activities were once prime material for every scandal magazine…and they were probably right.

I finally moved out of that apartment building because it was just too "wild" a place for me. There were loud parties almost every night and the walls were thin. But, the straw that really broke the camel's back was the Saturday afternoon that a half dozen police cars descended on the building and, with guns drawn, raided one of the apartments on a lower floor, breaking up a narcotics operation.

I found a nice single apartment in Hollywood at Franklin and Argyle, and moved.

During the period I was at Retail Credit, I wrote, produced directed and financed *Genesis*. This was a short film, shot and edited by Ted V. Mikels (*The Astro Zombies*) and narrated by John Carradine, which (I'd hoped) would serve as a "calling card" and get me work as a director in Hollywood.

It didn't.

Also, for fifteen hundred dollars, I purchased *Journey From a Desolate Place*, an original screenplay by Douglas Fleming, which I planned to package and shoot in Seattle where I hoped to get financing. That "package" included actors Nick Adams, a recent Oscar nominee for *Twilight of Honor*, Robert Conrad (pre-*The Wild, Wild West*) and one-time child star Gigi Perreau.

That didn't happen either.

I may have a talent for selling myself as a publicist...as a writer...as a stage director...or as a trustworthy person who can "do the job," but with the exception of Actor's Theatre, I've never been able to raise money. Not even a nickel.

Certainly the best thing that came out of the *Journey From a Desolate Place* experience was a friendship, albeit distant, with Gigi Perreau.

It has been well over forty years since I tried to put that project together, and I don't think that Gigi and I have met face-to-face more than once or twice since then. Perhaps we talked on the phone one or two times more than that.

Yet, in the fall of 2010, when I was in Los Angeles doing a book signing for *My Forty-Five Years in Hollywood...And How I Escaped Alive*, Gigi was there. That was a delightful surprise, and we've stayed in contact, via e-mail, ever since. She is a charming, lovely lady.

(I know you must be thinking that I'm skipping too quickly over the events in this chapter, and you're right. But, I warned you in the *Preface* that I would be doing this. I covered most of this material in much greater detail in my first memoir, so if you haven't done so already, I suggest that you put this book aside for the moment and read *My Forty-Five Years in Hollywood...And How I Escaped Alive* first.)

Now divorced, Terry had moved down to the Los Angeles area shortly after me and was living with her kids in Redondo Beach. As a result, though my apartment was in Hollywood, I was spending many evenings and weekends in the South Bay area where I managed to garner two directing assignments in local community theaters. Both earned me excellent reviews.

A Shot in the Dark by Harry Kurnitz, which served as the basis, but bears scant resemblance to the Peter Sellers "Inspector Clouseau" movie of the same name, was presented at the Hampton Playhouse and featured the enchanting Rita Willens, doing her second stage role, in the lead. Terry also had a supporting part in that production.

Then, over at the nearby Chapel Theatre in Torrance, run by Don Gish, a relative of Lillian and Dorothy, I directed a production of one of my all-time favorite plays, Herb Gardner's *A Thousand Clowns*. Of the staging, one newspaper critic commented: "*How two groups can put on the same play with different results is a real mystery. We saw* A Thousand

Clowns *done in theatre in the round and with well-known names from Hollywood in the leading roles and was not a bit impressed, but last Friday we saw it again at Chapel and came away raving about the perfect casting and how entertaining it was. Michael Druxman has secured a cast without a flaw and has molded them into an evening of solid enjoyment."*

In 1983, I was offered the opportunity to play "Murray Burns," the leading role in *A Thousand Clowns*, which was going to be presented at the Stage Door Theatre in Agoura Hills, the same theater that would produce the initial productions of my plays, *Gable* and *Tracy*. It's a project that I would really have liked to have done, primarily because my then fourteen year old son, David, was going to play "Nick," Murray's nephew.

Ultimately, I decided not to do the production. It had been over twenty years since I'd acted on stage and, although the Murray Burns character was quite a bit like myself, I no longer had the confidence to trod the boards, particularly in such an important role. Indeed, while I was pondering whether to do the project or not, I began experiencing nightmares that I hadn't had for years; actor's nightmares of appearing on stage and not knowing what play I was doing, or worse yet, appearing on stage naked.

Of course, had the play been *Oh! Calcutta* or *Hair*, those nightmares would have just been…dreams.

I was definitely a proud father sitting in the audience of *A Thousand Clowns*. My son was superb.

After *A Thousand Clowns* at the Chapel, I would not direct another play for many years.

It's not that I didn't have opportunities to direct. There were plenty of those for me in community theatre, but there was no money to be made doing these amateur productions. And, people in the motion picture business did not drive all the way down to the South Bay in search of directing talent.

In the words of Richard Nixon: "Let me make this perfectly clear…"

I like money.

I *really* like money…at least enough to support my lifestyle.

Money, however, is *not* the reason I wanted to scale the high, barbed wire-covered walls of the entertainment industry.

Like everybody else with an artistic bent, I wanted to do "the work".

More specifically, I wanted to make movies.

If all I desired to do was community theatre, I could have stayed in Seattle and, in all probability, done quite well there. I would have been a "big fish in a small pond".

But, I wanted to be "a professional"; to make my living in the business and, back in the 1960s, that meant moving to either New York or Hollywood. (*It still does.*) And, Hollywood has a much warmer climate.

"Making a living" became an issue shortly after *A Thousand Clowns* closed. My superiors at Retail Credit were not too happy that, following late night rehearsals, I was coming into work every morning bleary-eyed. Then, during the tragic Watts Riots of 1965, tensions peaked when I refused to drive down into the South Los Angeles area, my regular territory, and conduct insurance investigations.[1]

I didn't work for Retail Credit much longer.

I got a job writing professional résumés, and while I was doing that, I met a former Hollywood publicist, also writing résumés. He explained to me how the Hollywood public relations game worked, in particular what a client expected of his press agent and the kind of fees that they paid for that service.

I couldn't believe it. Those fees were huge, and the amount of work that a publicist had to do to earn them was minimal. Essentially, you wrote and planted news releases and pitched interviews, both of which I'd done plenty of times for my own projects back in Seattle. I'd even placed stories in the Hollywood trade papers when I was producing *Genesis*.

I wish I could remember his name so I could have dedicated this book to him, because that guy sparked an idea in my brain. I was going to open a low budget public relations office; one with a minimum overhead and whose services almost anybody in the motion picture business could afford.

It would be the "Wal-Mart" of publicity services.

I know. Wal-Mart didn't exist yet, but you get the idea.

I took small ads in *Daily Variety* and *The Hollywood Reporter*, "A Press Agent for $25.00". On the day that they ran, the phone started ringing and I was in business.

That business would continue to support me well for almost thirty years.

---

1. Late on Friday night, perhaps the worst night of the riots, I was driving up the Harbor Freeway, on my way home from Terry's Redondo Beach apartment. I glanced over toward the east, and it looked like the entire city of Los Angeles was in flames. It was a frightening, unforgettable sight.

7

The Publicist

THE PUBLIC RELATIONS FIRM of Michael B. Druxman and Associates was a success from its first day. Of course, there were really no "Associates," just me with a rented electric typewriter and a mimeograph machine in a one-room office. I was on the second floor of an old colonial-style building on Sunset Boulevard in Hollywood, between Highland and LaBrea.

I figured that "Associates" gave the business a tinge of class.

In my previous memoir, I wrote about how The Publicists Guild was upset about the "A Press Agent for $25.00" ads that I was running, and I also wrote about some of my early clients (Sal Mineo, David Winters, Pat Harrington, Stanley Rubin, Paul Francis Webster, etc.), so I won't repeat those stories here.

READ THE OTHER BOOK!

Some of the people I represented during that first year may not have been as influential in my career as those I previously wrote about, but they are definitely etched into my memory. Indeed, the fees they paid me were nothing to shout about, yet being a lifelong movie buff, just working with them was reward enough.

For example, you may or may not recognize the name "Reed Hadley," but if you enjoy movies of the 1940s and 1950s, you would certainly recognize his face and his distinctive voice, which can be heard narrating such classic films as *Guadalcanal Diary*, in which he also appeared, *The House on 92nd Street*, *Boomerang* and *13 Rue Madeleine*. Television viewers will remember him best as "Captain Braddock" in the popular 1951-53 series, *Racket Squad*.

When Reed came to me, he was frustrated. He hadn't worked much during the past few years and he was particularly unhappy with his last job, the role of mobster "Hymie Weiss" in *The St. Valentine's Day Massacre* (1967), a film directed by my future boss, Roger Corman. "Would you believe," Reed said to me, "with my trained voice, I don't have one line in the picture?"

He was right. He appeared in two scenes. In one, he was sitting in a car and waved to somebody and, in the other; he's shot down in the street.

I felt badly for Reed, but from a business standpoint, I would come to understand why his once busy career was winding down. Sometimes a familiar face (or voice) becomes *too* familiar, and producers want a "fresh" look for their films or television shows. Seasoned actors, also, usually cost more money than talented newcomers and, unless that veteran performer is a recognizable "name," a producer has to wonder if paying the higher salary is worth it.

Reed stayed with me for three months. Unfortunately, there was little I could do for him, so we parted ways.

Another actor who shared Reed Hadley's problem was James Griffith.

You probably don't recognize the name, but if you "Google" him, you will certainly recognize the face, since he played supporting and bit roles in innumerable movies (*Tribute to a Bad Man*, *Raintree County*) and television shows from the late 1940s through the early 1980s. One newspaper interview I set up for him, in fact, was headlined: "*I Know Him! What's His Name?*"

"If I can get one job per month," Jim told me, "that will cover my nut."[1]

I can't be positive, but I believe that Griffith played Abraham Lincoln on film more often than any other actor, usually in the opening scene of a "B" Western. As the 16th President, he would be discussing some aspect of the westward expansion with a senator or cabinet member, then the scene would end with Honest Abe saying something like, "If you gentlemen would excuse me, Mrs. Lincoln and I have a date for the theatre."

Jim stayed with me for about a year.

Don Keefer was still another actor who played countless small roles in movies (e.g. *Butch Cassidy and the Sundance Kid*) and on television, but whose major claim to fame is that he originated the role of "Bernard"

---

1. Director Robert Aldrich (*The Dirty Dozen*) once advised up-and-coming actor Bruce Davison (*Willard*): "You can be a leading man and have a career that lasts six or seven years, or you can become a character actor and put your kids through college."

in Arthur Miller's *Death of a Salesman* and continued in the part for the play's entire Broadway run. He also repeated the role in the 1951 movie version with Fredric March.

When Don wasn't working in Hollywood, he traveled to various cities around the country, performing a one-person play he'd written about Russian playwright Anton Chekhov. "When I do these shows," he mused, "the people always pick me up when I first arrive in town, but they never drive me back to the airport when I've finished. When they're done with you, you're on your own."

In fact, he said that, if he ever wrote his autobiography, he would call it *They Never Drive You Back*.

One day, I visited Keefer on the set of *The Iron Horse*, a Western TV series starring Dale Robertson, in which Don was playing a crooked lawyer who gets shot in the final scene. "It's always simpler to kill off the bad guy," he said, explaining his violent demise. "That way, there's no need for explanations; no need for a scene where I'm led away in handcuffs."

That was a good tip; something that this writer remembered.

For a short time, I also represented Swiss mountaineer Norman Dyhrenfurth, who in 1963 led the first American expedition that reached the top of Mount Everest, and then there was the seven-foot tall young man, whose name escapes me, that played all of the rubber-suited monsters on the *Voyage to the Bottom of the Sea* television series.

An even more offbeat, albeit amusing, client was Aram Katcher.

Born in Turkey, he was short, balding, colorful and a definite Peter Lorre type. Although he had an ego to surpass that of Orson Welles and dreamed of making his own films, Aram was really a part-time actor who played mostly bits, earning his day-to-day living as a ladies hairdresser. He did, in fact, own a successful salon on Wilshire Boulevard, just west of Fairfax. "Get to work," he would jokingly shout at his female employees, "or I'm going to turn this place into a whorehouse!"

Aram bore a remarkable resemblance to Napoleon Bonaparte and had been cast as the French emperor two or three times on film, most notably in the final scene of MGM's *Scaramouche* (1952) with Stewart Granger, Janet Leigh and Eleanor Parker in which he had no dialogue.

When he came to me in 1967, he had recently finished filming an episode of *I Dream of Jeannie* with Barbara Eden. Once again, he'd played Napoleon.

Unfortunately, Aram hadn't endeared himself to the people on that series, particularly Claudio Guzman, director of the episode. As Barbara Eden would recall to me, the cast and crew were aghast when, in the middle of *several* takes, Katcher, unhappy with the way a scene was progressing, had usurped Guzman's authority and called "Cut!"

Aram wanted to do a major publicity push to promote his appearance on *Jeannie*, but the sad fact was that he was just playing a one or two-day role in a single episode of a well-established half-hour sitcom, and the press really wasn't that interested. I designed a trade ad and also arranged an interview or two, based on the dubious premise that Aram had played Napoleon more than any other actor, but that was about all that could be done for him.

The episode aired…was quickly forgotten…and that was that.

Some of the people who came to my office during those first few months were definitely on the "weird" side, like the fellow who was on vacation, visiting from the Midwest. Having seen my ad, he'd walked into my office unannounced, sat down and refused to leave until I helped him become a movie star.

"What acting experience do you have?" I asked.

"None," he said, "but all I need is for a producer to see me, and he'll see that I'm a special type."

The guy was probably right. Unfortunately, *One Flew Over the Cuckoo's Nest* was a decade away from being produced yet.

After about a half hour, Terry arrived at the office. We were married by then, and we had a date for lunch.

"Excuse me," I said to the fellow before Terry could open her mouth, "I have a lunch meeting with my client here, so I have to go."

"When will you be back?"

"Not sure," I fibbed. "I could be gone the rest of the day."

He grumbled a bit, but he left and I never saw him again.

On the other hand, whoever said I could recognize talent when I saw it?

One day, a husband and wife, both actors, walked into my office seeking representation. I thought the wife had possibilities, however although the husband had worked in community theatre and done some small parts on episodic television, I didn't think there was much I could do for him as a publicist.

It was a cordial meeting, but neither one became a client.

The couple would later divorce. The wife, Judy Farrell, became a respected television writer on *Port Charles*, a spin-off of *General Hospital*.

And, the husband?

He would go on to co-star in several television series, including *M*A*S*H*.

His name was Mike Farrell.

Dumb! Dumb! Dumb!

David F. Friedman was an exploitation film producer, a former carnival promoter, whose credits included *Blood Feast* (1963) and *Two Thousand Maniacs* (1964). He hired me about this same time to do a character/dialogue polish on a screenplay, *She Freak* (1967), which was really a thinly disguised remake of the Tod Browning classic, *Freaks* (1932).

If you ever see *She Freak*, you will not see my name on-screen, which could be a blessing. I was a bit too trusting back in those days to insist on a contract that guaranteed me writing credit…a mistake that I would not make again.

You live and learn.

Nevertheless, Dave Friedman and I remained on good terms. In 1970, he hired me to publicize a nudie movie he was producing, *Trader Hornee*. Scandalous when it was first released, it is incredibly innocent by today's standards.

The first "name" performer I represented was Daws Butler.

Who's Daws Butler?

Daws was "the Mel Blanc of television animation," the voice of Yogi Bear, Quick Draw McGraw and Huckleberry Hound, as well as several other cartoon characters. Frankly, I don't recall a lot about Daws, except that he was a short, friendly fellow, and when I booked him for a television appearance, he would bring along a hand puppet of either Huckleberry or Yogi, and they would contribute to the conversation.

Another voice actor, Don Messick, was a good friend of Butler's, and he became a client at the same time as Daws. Messick is probably best remembered as the voices of Boo Boo Bear, Ranger Smith, Ricochet Rabbit and Scooby-Doo.

I will be forever grateful to Don because he made it possible for me to meet one of my childhood idols, Bud Abbott, perhaps the greatest straight man the entertainment industry has ever known.

Don was doing various voices for the *Abbott & Costello* animated cartoon series, produced by Hanna/Barbera. The voice of Lou Costello was being recreated by Stan Irwin, but as part of his deal and despite the fact that the producers would have preferred using a professional voice artist, Abbott had insisted on playing himself. He was a trooper and wanted to work. I also assume that he needed the money, since it was no secret that the Internal Revenue Service had pretty much cleaned him out a few years before.

Abbott was much heavier than he appeared in films or television, and he used a walker. A warm, gracious man, we spent several minutes chatting during one of the session breaks. He particularly enjoyed recalling how he and Costello never stuck to the script as written.

Driving back to my office, I remembered something that my father had once said about Abbott and Costello: "Abbott would be nothing without Costello. He would starve to death."

Dad was wrong.

You may laugh at the comic, but the real key to a successful comedy team is the straight man. He's the one who controls the timing of the act, and it's his reaction to the comic's antics that actually evokes the laughs.

Among the people I interviewed when I was researching my one-person play on Clark Gable was veteran screenwriter John Lee Mahin (*Captains Courageous*, *Show Boat*, *Quo Vadis*, etc.). He'd written several Gable films, including *Mogambo* (1953), which co-starred Ava Gardner.

"You son-of-a-bitch," Gable had said after he'd read the script. "You gave Ava all the funny lines."

"That's right," Mahin replied. "But, the audience won't laugh until we cut to your reaction."

Think about it.

In spite of what the French say, was Jerry Lewis ever as funny after he broke up with Dean Martin?

And, as far as Lou Costello is concerned, after he broke up with Bud Abbott near the end of his career, he made some solo appearances on Steve Allen's television show, usually doing the same routines that he'd done with Abbott with a different partner…and they fell flat. The chemistry just wasn't there.

So, Dad…wherever you are…don't sell the straight man short.

8

Rock Hudson

THIS IS A STORY that I've only told to special friends and family or, on occasion, when I've been in a devilish mood and felt like "shocking" the person I was with.

It's an R-rated tale, so if you are easily offended, you might want to skip to the next chapter.

In Hollywood, the sizes of certain actors' cocks are legend. These enormous phalluses have been discussed in bedrooms, at cocktail parties, over business lunches and have even been written about in books.

Silent film star Clara Bow claimed that one time boy friend Gary Cooper "was hung like a horse."

Comedian Milton Berle used to joke about the size of his cock at Friars' Club roasts.

Actor John Ireland once read me a poem he'd written about the dimensions of his manhood, and it's said that when actor Forrest Tucker had had too much to drink and fell asleep in the locker room of his golf club, fellow members would come over and take a peek under the towel covering him in order to verify that the stories they'd heard were true.

They were.

On the other hand, according to Al Jolson, who saw him once in a locker room, Clark Gable, the "King of Hollywood," was *under* endowed.

Perhaps Jolson never forgave Gable when *Gone With The Wind* surpassed his picture, *The Singing Fool*, as the highest grossing movie of all time.

And, John Wayne? It's said that he had small feet.

Since none of these contenders ever stood next to each other while a judge used a tape measure to determine a winner, I guess there is no way to verify which one deserved the crown. But, according to many folks, the championship in "Hollywood's Biggest Cock" contest should definitely go to Rock Hudson.

And, I can personally assure you, without question, that these folks are probably right.

Oops!

I know what you're thinking.

"How the hell does Druxman know that unless…."

Well, you're right.

I did, but not in the way you might think.

I'll explain.

It was always an open secret in Hollywood that Rock Hudson was gay. Actually, that secret wasn't confined to Hollywood. I'd first heard about the actor's sexual preference back in Seattle when I was in high school.

But, like the love affair between Spencer Tracy and Katharine Hepburn, also an open Hollywood secret, nobody in the film business paid much mind to these potential scandals because, in contrast to some of their colleagues, these stars were smart enough to keep their private lives private. Indeed, Rock Hudson was a likable guy and he presented a macho and romantic image on screen. He was also a major box-office star, so Universal Pictures, where he was under contract, did everything they could to protect that moneymaking image and Hudson made it a definite point to publicly stay "in the closet".

However, hearing reports of Rock's physical endowments from other guys in the Universal locker room, actresses under contract to the studio often quipped: "What a waste!"

My first contact with Rock Hudson was in 1952 when he came to Seattle's Orpheum Theater for the premiere of *Bend of the River*, a Jimmy Stewart Western, in which he'd appeared. He was at the theater to sign autographs, along with co-stars Julie Adams and Lori Nelson.

I was eleven-years-old, and in my autograph collecting mode, so I was almost first in line to get the signatures of these three stars.

Years went by. I saw many Rock Hudson movies (*The Lawless Breed*, *Giant* and *Lover Come Back* were particular favorites), and I kept hearing the titillating gossip about him.

After I started my publicity business, a friend suggested that I might make some good show business contacts, and even pick up a client or two, if I joined the Beverly Hills Health Club on Santa Monica Boulevard, a place where many name actors (e.g. Peter Falk) were members.

People who know me are aware that I'm not a big fan of exercise. I know I should do it, that it would be good for me, but I find lifting weights, walking a treadmill or riding a stationary bike to be boring. I avoid it whenever possible. During the past few years, my exercise has been limited to walking my dog around the block or pulling weeds in my yard.

But, back then, I was trying to build my business and if that meant that I spent an hour or so at the Beverly Hills Health Club twice a week, so be it.

I joined the club. I lifted weights. I swam in the pool. I walked the treadmill.

I didn't pick up any publicity clients.

I did enjoy the club's steam room. Following a workout, I would relax in there for fifteen or twenty minutes, and then after a shower, feel totally refreshed.

A nice thing about this club was that you did not have to bring your own gym clothes. The club furnished terrycloth shorts for you to wear, as well as sandals and towels. It was a high-class operation.

One day, I walked into the steam room and saw that there was one other person in there. The newspaper he was reading hid his face.

I sat on the bench across from him and, after minute or two; I looked at the headline on the opposite side of his newspaper. As my eyes moved down the page, I also noticed that this guy was wearing neither terrycloth shorts nor a towel. He was naked.

Obviously, I saw his penis.

But, this was not an ordinary penis.

This was *a PENIS*!

What can I say?

I had no idea they came in XXXXX Large.

And, Jewish?

As I averted my eyes, I saw that this man was looking at me, and smiling.

Yes, it was Rock Hudson.

I guess he *wasn't* Jewish.

I didn't say a word. Neither did he.

I looked away, and he went back to reading his newspaper.

After a couple of minutes, I nonchalantly left the steam room, and except for visiting a client on set of Hudson's television series, *McMillan & Wife*, many years later, I never saw him in person again.

I know. It's not an earth-shattering story, but:
XXXXX Large!
Wow!

9

Gale Gordon, Composers & Directors

"*Eventually, you will lose all of your clients.*"
My late good friend, syndicated newspaper columnist, James Bacon, once made that frightening pronouncement to me.

Jim wasn't criticizing my work as a publicist. He knew that the Hollywood press respected me and that I did a good job for my clients. And, he wasn't suggesting that all of my clients were going to walk out on me en masse.

No, he was referring to the realities of the publicity business.

People and their careers change. No matter how long a client has been with you, there may come a time when they either no longer need or can afford a publicist.

Or, conversely, the publicist might realize that he is "tapped out" on that particular client. Creatively, there is nothing more that he can do for him.

Bob Hope and Frank Sinatra had been with their respective publicists for many years, yet late in their lives they switched. Hope hired Sinatra's publicist and vice versa. I guess that both stars felt that they needed fresh eyes on their careers.

During the thirty plus years that I was in the publicity game, clients came and went, and, when the need arose, some came back again. Most of them I got along with, but some I didn't. A few fired me and I even fired a couple. Several of them became and remain good friends.

Although I had picked up a few "name" clients prior to meeting him, my publicity business really didn't take off until after I started representing producer Stanley Rubin (*The Narrow Margin, River of No Return, The President's Analyst, White Hunter, Black Heart*), who would become my friend and "mentor".

Happy with the work I had done for him, Stanley not only recommended my services to his friends in the business, like television producer Norman Felton (*The Man From U.N.C.L.E.*), he also put me in touch with his agent, Harold Rose, who represented producers and directors, and was partnered with Marc Newman, brother of Alfred and Lionel Newman, and one of the top agents for film composers in Hollywood. Over the years, these two men sent me many well-known clients, which, in fact, turned my fledgling publicity office into one of the most respected boutique agencies in town.

[One small caveat: Not that it makes a difference to the veracity of these anecdotes, but with some of the clients that I mention in this chapter, I'm not one hundred percent sure that they actually came to me via Harold Rose or Marc Newman. I believe they did, but my memory of those events is not as sharp as it used to be. Other clients may have referred some of them. I don't really recall. However, talking about these talented people in this chapter seems to be a good fit.]

Among the composers from Newman's stable that I represented were John Williams (*Jaws, Star Wars*), Ernest Gold (*Exodus*), Johnny Mandel (*M*A*S*H*), Fred Karlin (*Lovers and Other Strangers*) and Leith Stevens.

Stevens was a nice, soft-spoken, rather interesting man. Probably best remembered for his jazz scores, he had composed music for a variety of movie genres. His credits included *Destination Moon* (1950), *The Wild One* (1953), *The Garment Jungle* (1957), *But Not For Me* (1959) and even *It Happened at the World's Fair* (1963), the movie in which I'd appeared with Elvis Presley. He was also one of the first composers to utilize electronic music in films.

During the interviews I set up for him, Leith would often bring the journalist over to his office and demonstrate his Moog synthesizer. At the time I represented him, he was in charge of the music department at Paramount Television.

One afternoon, I received a phone call from a Paramount publicist with whom I often worked. "Have you heard about Leith?" he asked.

"No. What about Leith?"

"He died."

Earlier that day, Leith's wife had been killed in an automobile accident. Upon hearing the news, he had suffered a fatal heart attack.

Leith Stevens was sixty years old.

Another client sent to me by Newman was Manos Hadjidakis, a revered Greek composer who had won the Academy Award in 1960 for writing the title song for *Never on Sunday*, which had been directed by Jules Dassin and had starred his wife, Melina Mercouri. In 1967, the hit film had been adapted into a Broadway musical, *Ilya Darling*, also directed by Dassin, starring Ms. Mercouri, and with Hadjidakis writing the score with lyricist Joe Darion (*Man of La Mancha*).

Hadjidakis was in Hollywood to write the score for *Blue* (1968), a Paramount Western starring Terence Stamp, and, back in New York, he had just been nominated for a Tony Award for his contribution to *Ilya Darling*.

My job was to set up a press conference, in which he would *refuse* the Tony nomination.

Remember, this was 1968, two years before George C. Scott made headlines by refusing the Oscar for *Patton* and four years prior to Marlon Brando doing the same thing for *The Godfather*, so this act by Hadjidakis was rather unusual and definitely newsworthy.

Truthfully, I never really understood why he was doing this, except that he was unhappy with the finished production, which except for Ms. Mercouri's performance had not received good reviews from the New York critics.

Also, truthfully, I thought that Hadjidakis was nuts to refuse the nomination, but I was hired to set up a press conference, and that's what I did.

Being a native of Greece, Hadjidakis was not that fluent in English, thus he was always accompanied by Stathis Giallelis, who had a key role in *Blue*, but is best remembered for playing the leading role in Elia Kazan's *America, America* (1963). He served as Hadjidakis' translator.

I got plenty of press for Hadjidakis, but he could have saved his money. *Ilya Darling* did not win any Tony Awards.

Marc Newman had one client who was not in the music business, Gale Gordon, Lucille Ball's favorite foil on her various television series.

Gale became a client and stayed with me for many years.

He was so unlike his angry, frustrated, on-screen persona. When fans asked him why he was always so mean to Lucy, his stock reply was, "I only get mad for money."

Gale was an easy client to represent. He expected little from me, just to set an occasional interview and to send out photographs and press materials when he was doing a play in dinner or regional theatre, which he did frequently when *Here's Lucy!* was not filming. *Never Too Late* was the stage play that he did most often.

He was a generous man, always willing to donate his time to a worthy cause. On one occasion, I set him to make an appearance at a fund-raising event for the Santa Ynez Branch of the Chumash Indian Reservation, located in the mountains above Santa Barbara.

Gale drove up to Santa Barbara, stayed in a local hotel (on his own dime), then although I told him that he didn't have to do it, he insisted on paying our admission into the event where he sat for two hours autographing photos, and listening to fans ask insensitive questions, such as, "Why isn't Lucy here?"

Gale Gordon may have been a kind, gentle and likable man, but he was not a good interview subject. Indeed, his own agent, Marc Newman, said he was "boring" to talk to, and by the time he became my client, virtually every newspaperman in town had interviewed him more than once over the years, so they knew they were not going to get any hot copy out of him. At times, I literally had to beg them to sit down with Gale again.

When he heard that I was writing a book on Basil Rathbone, Gale asked me why I hadn't asked him for an interview. He then informed me that he had played "Inspector Lestrade" on the *Sherlock Holmes* radio show, and proceeded to relate several amusing Rathbone and Nigel Bruce anecdotes that I wound up using in my book, *Basil Rathbone: His Life and His Films* (1975).

Later, I set him to talk about Rathbone at a dinner meeting of the local Sherlock Holmes Society where, on the dais, I was seated next to writer Ray Bradbury, with whom I had an enjoyable chat.

That was one of the wonderful perks about being a publicist and accompanying my celebrity clients to various events. I got to rub shoulders with some fascinating and important people who I would never have met otherwise.

A few years ago, the publisher of BearManor Media asked me if I would be interested in writing a book about Gale. "There's really no book there," I said, turning down the assignment. "Aside from a filmography, what would you write? He did his job, made no scandalous headlines, and lived a quiet life with his wife in the desert town of Borrego Springs."

Gale's approach to acting was much like that of Arthur Treacher, Hollywood's quintessential English butler, who once described his job as: "You say the words. You take the money. You go home."

The first two clients that I got through Harold Rose were directors whose work I greatly admired.

In my first memoir, I devoted an entire chapter to Edward Dmytryk, director of such classic films as *Murder, My Sweet*; *Crossfire*; *The Caine Mutiny*; *Raintree County*; and *The Young Lions*, but since that book was published, I've recalled a few anecdotes that Eddie shared with me about some of the iconic stars with whom he worked that I will now share with you.

According to Eddie, *Murder, My Sweet* (1944) starring Dick Powell as Raymond Chandler's "Philip Marlowe" was the movie that started Hollywood's vogue toward *film noir*. True, *The Maltese Falcon* (1941) preceded it, but that picture did not begin the trend.

Dmytryk did not want Dick Powell as the star of his movie. Indeed, he was "horrified" when his bosses at RKO told him that the musical-comedy star (*42ⁿᵈ Street*) had been cast as Raymond Chandler's "hard-boiled" detective. Powell had signed a deal with the studio with the proviso that his first role would be a dramatic one, and Eddie was stuck with him. "Well, it will be a challenge," he rationalized to himself after he recovered from the shock.

It was a challenge well met. Both Powell and the picture were major hits.

When Eddie first started directing *The Caine Mutiny* (1954), star Humphrey Bogart came to him one day and asked him for his input on a particular line of dialogue. Dmytryk explained the line to him, upon which Bogart replied: "I knew that. I just wanted to know if you did, too." After that, star and director got along fine.

For *Soldier of Fortune* (1955), Dmytryk and star Clark Gable went on location to Hong Kong. One night, Eddie was waiting for Gable in the hotel dining room where they were going to have dinner. In the booth next to him, he overheard a woman talking, "I hear that Clark Gable's in the hotel. He's no big deal, just a big hunk who is probably full of himself because he's a movie star." The woman continued on like that for several minutes.

Then, Gable walked into the room. The woman looked at him. He smiled at her and, as Eddie described it, "she fainted dead away."

Eddie made two movies with Spencer Tracy, *Broken Lance* (1954) and *The Mountain* (1956). On one of those films, a young actor (who will remain nameless) started giving the director a bad time because he felt he didn't have the proper motivation to follow the script, which had him walking through a door. This discussion went on for a bit until an irked Tracy interrupted with: "Your motivation for walking through the goddamn door is that it's the only way that you can get into the goddamn room. Now, shut up and let's shoot the scene."

I love that story. It always reminds me of an incident that happened when I was directing *The Doorway* with Roy Scheider for Roger Corman in Ireland in 1999.

We were shooting a scene in a bedroom that, in the finished picture, would be split into two parts by a brief cutaway to another scene. For the second half of the scene, I told an actor that I wanted him to stand on the other side of the bed.

"What's my motivation for walking over there?" he wanted to know.

"You don't need a motivation," I said. "There has been a passage of time from the first part of the scene. We don't need to see you actually walk over there."

That didn't satisfy him. He didn't seem to understand that I, as the director, had the movie's complete mosaic in my head. I knew how these scenes would edit together on the screen, yet he insisted on debating the issue. Precious time was wasting.

Finally, I said to him: "Your motivation is that that's where I want you to be."

At which time, an amused Roy Scheider chimed in: "In other words, your motivation is your paycheck."

The actor moved to the other side of the bed.

My favorite Western star has always been Randolph Scott, so in the late 1960s, when Harold Rose sent me Budd Boetticher to be a client, I was delighted. Boetticher had directed seven of Scott's most revered films, including *Seven Men From Now*, *The Tall T*, *Ride Lonesome* and *Comanche Station*.

One of those seven pictures, *Westbound* (1959), Boetticher actually campaigned to direct. Scott owed another movie to Warner Brothers but, with the exception of *Seven Men From Now*, most of the films that he'd made at that studio were not in the same league as the ones he'd done with Boetticher at Columbia, so Budd went out to that Burbank-based studio and offered to direct *Westbound* for one dollar.

"Why would you do that?" he was asked.

"Because I want to protect my star."

They hired Budd to direct *Westbound*, but they did pay him his regular salary.

Apparently never easy to work with, Budd was a maverick and had been on the outs with the Hollywood studios for several years when we first met. He'd been living in Mexico and was working (i.e., seeking further financing) on *Arruza*, a documentary feature about acclaimed late bullfighter Carlos Arruza that he'd started shooting in 1959. Jason Robards had recorded the narration for the picture, but Budd was not happy with his work. "He was drunk when he did it," said Budd, who had his own drinking problem.

When *Arruza* was finally released in 1972, the narrator was Anthony Quinn.

Budd was also talking about suing Universal Pictures. Prior to our meeting, he had sold them a screenplay entitled *Two Mules for Sister Sara*. He claimed that his deal stipulated that he was to direct the picture, but that the studio had reneged.

I don't know the terms, but evidently the matter was settled without bloodshed. *Two Mules for Sister Sara* starring Shirley MacLaine and Clint Eastwood was released in 1970 with Don Siegel as director. Albert Maltz got sole screenplay credit and Boetticher was credited with the "original story".

Budd would only write and direct one more feature, *A Time For Dying* (1969), a forgettable Western. Its only distinction is that it marked the final screen appearance of Audie Murphy, who played a small cameo role as Jesse James.

I was out of touch with Budd for many years, but we got together in Malibu one afternoon in 2001 (shortly before he passed away) when he added his signature to a lobby card from *The Tall T*, previously autographed by Randolph Scott, which is now framed and proudly displayed on a wall in my home.

Short in stature, but a sought-after director of action movies, George Sherman's career dated back to the 1930s when he helmed "B" westerns starring Gene Autry and John Wayne. In the 1940s and 1950s, he worked at Universal and other studios, directing Errol Flynn in *Against All Flags*, Rory Calhoun and Piper Laurie in *Dawn at Socorro*, Tony Curtis in *Johnny Dark* and Van Heflin and Joanne Woodward in *Count Three and Pray*.

He was also a producer, his most notable credits wearing that hat being *The Comancheros* (1961) with John Wayne and the *Daniel Boone* television series with Fess Parker.

I didn't meet Sherman face-to-face for many months after he hired me via Harold Rose. He was in Florida producing the *Gentle Ben* television series for Ivan Tors Productions, which starred Dennis Weaver and young Clint Howard, who would much later appear in two movies that I wrote, *Cheyenne Warrior* and *Dillinger and Capone*.

Since we really didn't have much interaction while he was producing that series, I don't have any vivid memories of Sherman during that period, except that he was friendly and he did send me other clients.

However, a few years later, Sherman hired me again when he was chosen by John Wayne to direct *Big Jake* (1971), which was to co-star Maureen O'Hara, Richard Boone, Patrick Wayne (son of "the Duke") and Christopher Mitchum (Robert's son), who would later become my publicity client for a short period of time.

"This is a big break for me," Sherman told me over lunch at the Hollywood Brown Derby, "and I want to make the most of it." He also revealed at that meeting that he'd tried to talk Wayne out of casting both his son and young Mitchum, his thinking being that those two roles were strong enough to attract other, more important name actors. Wayne didn't agree.

Originally titled *The Million Dollar Kidnapping*, the picture would shoot in Mexico, where Sherman was not a happy camper. In a later interview with *Variety*, he complained about the production crews in Mexico, and how they were not as efficient as the crews he had worked with in the United States.

That interview did not endear him to Wayne's company, which often filmed south of the border. A few days later, *Variety* ran a follow-up story in which Wayne's people disputed Sherman's claims, thereby averting a possible "international incident." Or, at least, a less friendly reception the next time an American crew wanted to work in Mexico.

Big Jake may not be in the same league as *Red River* or *The Searchers*, but it is definitely an entertaining action Western. This would be the last feature that Sherman would direct prior to his passing in 1991.

I'm not sure if director Paul Landres came to me because Harold Rose represented him, or because he was also under contract to Ivan Tors and had worked with Sherman. Perhaps both men were instrumental in his becoming my publicity client.

I do know that I liked Paul and enjoyed working with him.

Formerly an editor, Paul Landres had been directing since the late 1940s, mostly "B" movies and episodic television. He worked in many genres, westerns, thrillers, horror, but when he became my client, he was under contract to direct every other episode of *Daktari*, a popular family adventure series starring Marshall Thompson, set in Africa, but actually filmed at Africa USA, an animal compound located just north of Los Angeles. Prior to that, he'd directed many episodes of Ivan Tors' *Flipper* series.

Although it was a bit of a schlep from my office, I always looked forward to visiting the stunning *Daktari* location, which was filled with all kinds of animals: lions, tigers, antelopes, elephants, plus Judy, the chimpanzee. I lunched with Paul out there often and, on one occasion, got reacquainted with episode guest star Sterling Holloway, with whom I'd worked (behind the scenes) at the Cirque Playhouse in Seattle during my high school days. (Actually, I don't think that he really remembered me, even though I'd picked him up at his hotel and drove him to the theater on several occasions.)

Paul Landres is a perfect example of how type casting cannot only hurt the career of an actor, but also a director.

He may not have been in the same league as a John Ford, Alfred Hitchcock or even an Edward Dmytryk or Budd Boetticher, but Paul was a good, efficient television director who knew his job and did it well. Yet, after *Daktari* was cancelled, he had difficulty getting further work. Despite all the other shows that he'd done prior to *Daktari*, the industry now considered him to be an "animal director," and since there were no new animal shows filming, he wasn't being hired.

From the cancellation of *Daktari* in 1968 to his death in 2001, Paul would only direct four more segments in episodic television.

I once asked another client, television director Gerald Mayer and the nephew of MGM's Louis B. Mayer, what it was like directing animals. He had just finished directing an episode of *Tarzan* with Ron Ely. "Nothing to it," he said. "I just tell the trainer that I want the chimpanzee to do this or that, and the trainer makes the chimp do this or that."

Simple, huh?

10

Comedians & Other Clients

THERE'S AN AXIOM IN SHOW BUSINESS: No matter how big a star might become, talent changes. It comes and goes.

Yet, management doesn't change. The talent agencies, public relations firms, personal and business managers are always there, ready to represent the next up-and-comer.

Sadly, today's George Clooney, Brad Pitt or Johnny Depp will, someday, likely follow in the footsteps of George Raft, Alan Ladd or Robert Taylor, once major movie stars who fell from grace after a few years in the spotlight. All it takes is just one or two box-office flops.

Over the years, I represented many people who, at one time, were "hot"; even the "hottest name in the business."

When he was on *77 Sunset Strip*, Edd "Kookie" Byrnes was adored by virtually every teenage girl in America, including my wife, Sandy, who confesses that her bedroom walls were covered with his photographs.[1] But, after the series left the air, acting assignments were few and far between for Edd. For a time, he moved to Italy where he and other former American television stars, like Guy Madison (*Wild Bill Hickock*), could make a good living appearing in "spaghetti Westerns".

While he was living there, Edd saw one of my ads, wrote to me, and then we got together after he moved back to Hollywood a few months later. Although I was able to get him plenty of press and book him on talk shows (e.g. *The Donald O'Connor Show*), the jobs he really wanted did not materialize and we, eventually, parted ways.

---

1. In 2010, Sandy finally got to meet her one-time idol when I introduced her to Edd at a celebrity autograph show we were doing together in Chicago.

In 1978, Byrnes did make a minor short-lived comeback when he played the Dick Clark-like television host in the hit movie, *Grease*.

Another client I represented for a time was actor Tom Drake, certainly best remembered as Judy Garland's "boy next door" in *Meet Me in St. Louis*.

Tom had been under contract to Metro-Goldwyn-Mayer for most of the 1940s, and, aside from the Judy Garland classic, the studio had given their young leading man prominent roles in a number of other major films (e.g. *The Green Years*, *Words and Music*). He continued to work fairly regularly as a free-lance actor in the 1950s (e.g. *Raintree County*, *Warlock*) and beyond, but the roles he got became less significant.

Having a problem with alcohol does not enhance an actor's looks... or work.

When I represented Tom, which as I recall, was in the late 1970s, he was doing an occasional guest shot on episodic television. I found him to be a likable gentleman, quite soft-spoken, even shy. He told me how he had "blown his big opportunity" after he'd left Metro by not signing with a major theatrical agency, but instead going with a smaller agent, who said he had a film for him that was to start shooting immediately.

Unfortunately, that picture never materialized.

Publicity-wise, there was not a lot that I could do for Tom beyond getting him an occasional mention in the trade papers when he got a job, and the fact that (on his own) he took out a trade ad announcing that he was also selling used cars, did not help his image.

The truth is that, by the time he came to me, Tom Drake's "time" had passed. I attended his funeral in 1982, and, I believe, that the only person there from his MGM days was his *Meet Me In St. Louis* co-star, Margaret O'Brien.

Brooklyn-born comedian Stanley Myron Handelman became an instant star in the late 1960s when he made a series of appearances on various television variety programs, such as *Dean Martin Presents the Golddiggers*, *The Tonight Show with Johnny Carson* and *The Ed Sullivan Show*. Wearing his signature cap and glasses, Stanley would crack up audiences with his absurd observations about life (e.g. *"I just got up from a sick bed. I don't know what's wrong with it—it just lies there."*).

Stanley was living in Los Angeles and he was, apparently, unhappy that his New York-based personal manager was dragging his feet about moving to the West Coast. Another manager phoned me, asking me if I would like to be Stanley's publicist. Of course, I said "yes."

I don't recall exactly how long I represented Stanley, but it was for the better part of a year. We got along well together, and I did get him a lot of press.

However, the relationship went south after his New York manager finally moved to Los Angeles. This guy's hostility to me was evident from the start. "You will never speak directly to my client," he decreed at our first meeting. "If you have something to say to him, you will go through me."

I think this guy considered me to be a threat, since I'd been introduced to Stanley via another manager who might well have wanted to take over representation of the comedian. The truth is that I had never met this other manager before he'd called me, and I don't recall that I ever had dealings with him since.

The New York manager continued to be nasty to me, but to his credit, when Stanley was booked as the opening act for Frank Sinatra at Caesar's Palace, he agreed to bring me over to Las Vegas to insure that our mutual client got his fair share of publicity. That's not an easy task to accomplish when the headliner is Sinatra, but I did it. The afternoon of that opening night, I saw to it that Stanley sat down with James Bacon, UPI's Vernon Scott and all the other out-of-town journalists.

Sitting in the empty showroom, watching Sinatra rehearse his act was certainly a memorable experience. He was definitely a "hands on" performer. Several times, he walked out into the empty auditorium, moving around the room, making sure that the lighting design was exactly right. Is it any wonder that he was known as the "Chairman of the Board"?

Stanley's first meeting with Sinatra was a bit unsettling.

He'd arrived in Las Vegas a day early and, as he was checking into the hotel, he spotted Sinatra walking through the lobby. The scrawny-sized comedian approached the show business icon and was about to tap him on the shoulder when one of Sinatra's brawny bodyguards shouted. "Don't touch him!"

"I thought I was going to have a heart attack," Stanley told me. "Then, Sinatra turned around, recognized me and smiled…and I knew everything was okay."

After the opening night show, I joined Stanley and his then-wife upstairs at Sinatra's private party where the gracious host greeted us warmly, introducing us to his other guests, such as Burt Lancaster, Yul Brynner,

Rod Steiger and Sammy Davis, Jr., who I was already acquainted with, since we were both fellow film buffs. It was quite an evening.

About a month later, I was in my office when I got a phone call from Stanley's New York manager. "You're fired," he said.

"Why?" I asked, somewhat surprised...but not really.

"Because that's the way I want it," then he hung up.

Within a year or two, with the exception of some club dates, Stanley pretty much disappeared from the public eye. The fact that he fired me had nothing to do with it.

Even more so than actors, the careers of most comedians have a limited life span, particularly when they possess a narrow bag of tricks. Somebody like Stanley may come upon the scene with a fresh comedic approach that captures an audience's fancy, but once they've been around for a while, unless they reinvent themselves, the public tires of them.

Milton Berle, Sid Caesar and even my childhood idols, Abbott and Costello, all became victims of the Zeitgeist.

On the other hand, icons like Bob Hope, Jack Benny and Groucho Marx remained popular until their deaths or until they were too ailing to work.

Why was that?

These men had public personas that people not only loved, but that also transcended the times.

Bob Hope may have made many movies and starred in God knows how many television specials, but he was, primarily, a monologist who kept a large staff of writers on salary that continually fed him one-liners on current events. He was also greatly admired for his generous, unending efforts to entertain our nation's military during both peacetime and in war.

I had the opportunity of interviewing Hope late in his life, and it was a pleasure. He particularly enjoyed relating the story about when he and Bing Crosby were filming *Road to Morocco*; a camel had spit in his eye.

Jack Benny, in contrast, surrounded himself with a delightful cast of stock characters (e.g. Eddie "Rochester" Anderson, Dennis Day, Mel Blanc, etc.) that audiences also adored, and whom he would play off of. Most of the time, he would give these other performers or his guest stars the punch line of a joke, but the audience would wait for his reaction, often just a silent gaze, before they laughed. Indeed, Benny's "cheapskate" persona was so familiar that the audience already knew how he was going to react, and would laugh in anticipation.

Of course, the classic Jack Benny moment is when he encounters a stick-up man, who demands, "Your money or your life!"

Long pause, evoking a huge laugh from the audience.

"I said, 'Your money or your life,'" the crook repeats.

Upon which Jack replies, "I'm thinking....I'm thinking."

As far as Groucho Marx is concerned, once he and his brothers broke up their act, he totally reinvented himself and became the purveyor of the most original and caustic one-liners in show business (e.g. "I didn't like the play, but then I saw it under adverse conditions—the curtain was up.").

When I was living in Calabasas during the 1990s, I often saw Stanley Myron Handelman, who was teaching comedy then, waiting for a bus on Topanga Canyon in Woodland Hills. Sometimes, if we were going in the same direction, I would give him a ride. He passed away in 2007.

During my career as a publicist, I represented several comedians. Among them were Rip Taylor, who used to mail me jokes written on toilet paper, and Jackie Vernon. However, the best-known funny man that I ever worked with was Jack Carter, a nightclub headliner; often referred to as "the comedian's comedian".

Brooklyn born, Jack was not only known for his rapid-fire delivery as a stand-up comic, but he was also a fine mimic, singer and actor, having received a Daytime Emmy nomination for an *ABC Afternoon Playbreak* episode in 1975. His versatility certainly contributed to his longevity in the business.

Carter became a client of mine through personal manager Raymond Katz who, over the years, also put me with actress Jessica Walter (*Grand Prix*, *Play Misty for Me*), singer Anita Kerr and Broadway composer Jule Styne (*Gypsy*, *Funny Girl*).

I liked Jack, but he was not an easy client to represent. He had a reputation for firing publicists every six months or so, but by some uncanny miracle, I wound up representing him for seven years, a world record.

How did I do it?

I just made sure that his name appeared in either *Daily Variety* or *The Hollywood Reporter* a minimum of once per week, even if it was just a one-line mention.

Jack was also known in town to be an "angry man". Columnist James Bacon always referred to him as "Hollywood's only sore winner."

I was witness to Jack's bursts of anger quite often. Driving with him behind the wheel was an experience never to be forgotten, as he would shout at almost every other driver on the road, with a "Schmuck! You're supposed to stop behind the crosswalk," or "Don't you dare steal my right-of-way."

I would sit in the passenger seat, petrified with fear at his reckless maneuvers, but also biting my lip so that I wouldn't laugh.

On stage, Jack was at his funniest when he was angry. Once, at the Riviera Hotel in Las Vegas, he snagged his tuxedo jacket on the proscenium just before he walked on stage. I could see that he was pissed, but he was hysterically funny that night.

Through Jack, I got to meet and mingle with a lot of people on Hollywood's "A" list, including Don Rickles, Anthony Quinn, Liza Minnelli, Joey Bishop, Jim Backus, Ricardo Montalban, Dick Martin (of Rowan and Martin) and even novelist and former cop, Joseph Wambaugh.

Two or three years into our relationship, Jack and I had a brief falling out. I don't remember what it was about, but in all probability, he was angry about something else and, as was his practice, he took it out on me. He even fired me.

Now, I was furious, because I felt he was treating me unfairly. I went back to my office and wrote him a scathing, albeit straightforward, letter. I said things to him in that "fuck you" letter that, I'm sure, no other publicist had ever articulated before…and then I mailed it.

Four days later, I received a brief note from Jack: "I forgive you for the letter. Come back!"

I guess he appreciated my honesty.

Jack and I had a more permanent falling out a few years later over a one-person play he'd contracted me to write about Al Jolson. That saga, as well as other Carter anecdotes, is detailed in my first memoir, so I won't repeat those stories here, except to say that after the *Jolson* incident, Jack was really angry and we didn't speak for years.

About six years ago, my wife, Sandy, encountered Jack in the waiting room of a doctor's office, and she introduced herself. He was quite friendly to her, and said: "Michael did some good work for me."

Since then, I've spoken to Jack on the phone once or twice. They were warm, friendly conversations. Despite any differences we might have had over the years, I still have only affable feelings toward him, and I'm proud of the fact that I was able to represent such a great talent.

Another client I represented, who I do not maintain warm feelings toward, was late actor Michael Conrad, best known for playing "Sgt. Phil Esterhaus" on the hit television series, *Hill Street Blues*.

I first became aware of Conrad when I saw him do a key part in the Burt Reynolds version of *The Longest Yard* (1974). As I continued to see him doing small roles in episodic television and in movies for the next few years, I couldn't help but wonder why this fine actor, who had a powerful screen presence, had never made it "big" in the business.

As I would often do with actors who attracted my interest (e.g. Steve Kanaly, Abe Vigoda), I eventually reached out to Conrad and suggested that we meet for lunch. He came into the office. We seemed to hit it off and he signed a standard one-year deal with me in which I would handle his publicity in exchange for five percent (5%) of his acting income for that period of time.

I set Conrad up for a couple of interviews, and then I booked him on the Arthritis Telethon, an annual fund-raiser that virtually every star in town (e.g. Bob Hope, Rosalind Russell, etc.) did at one time or another. In fact, one of my first publicity clients, Jack Rourke, produced the local telethon.

Conrad was set to appear and make a pitch on Saturday night around eight or nine o'clock. Divorced from Terry by then, I drove into town from the San Fernando Valley to be with him, and I took a date along with me.

When I arrived at the television studio, Michael approached me; extremely angry…a mood I would learn was not uncommon with him. In front of my date, he started his tirade. "How dare you book me on this show," he said. "They want me to ask for money."

"That's what telethons do," I tried to explain. "What did you think?"

"I don't know," he grumbled. "Not this."

After I explained to him that the donations were going to a worthy cause, he calmed down, went on camera, did the pitch…and he was terrible. He looked down the entire time he was on the air; never looked into the camera once.

Interestingly, when he gave his acceptance speeches after he won his two Emmys for *Hill Street Blues*, he never looked into the camera either.

During the few months he had been with me, Conrad had not had an acting job, thus I had not been paid anything for the work I had done for him. One day, he came into my office and said that he had just been hired for a television pilot and wanted to terminate his contract with me.

Frankly, I really didn't like the guy. He had a temper, was twice my size and I knew that if I tried to hold him to the agreement, we'd probably wind up in court. I told him that I would settle the agreement for one thousand dollars, payable that week. He agreed, and that was that.

Yes, it would have been nice to have a percentage of Michael Conrad's salary from *Hill Street Blues*, but I was well aware that there is really no way that you can hold a client if they don't want to be with you.

I may have lost a client, as well as thousands of dollars in publicity fees, but Conrad lost any respect that I might have had for him as a person of honor...not that he really cared about how I felt.

You may ask: "Wouldn't any client have done that? Either terminated or renegotiated your contract to save money on your services?"

Some would, but off-hand I can think of, at least, three clients who were with me on a percentage basis that did not cut me off when they came into a huge payday.

They are Steve Kanaly, Henry Darrow and Michael Ansara. All three paid me every nickel my percentage called for.

All of them are good friends and, more importantly, men of principle.

11

Dracula, Clemenza & Charles

WITH THE EXCEPTION OF MOVIES like *The Sixth Sense* or *The Others*, as well as some of the pictures made by Universal in the 1930s and 40s, I've never been a fan of the horror film, even though I've been hired on several occasions to write screenplays in that genre. Personally, I much prefer watching a good gangster movie or a classic Western.

Nevertheless, as with most movie buffs, I was fascinated with the mystique surrounding horror film stars. When I was a kid, visiting Los Angeles with my parents, I recall going up to Lon Chaney, Jr. at the Sportsman's Lodge and getting his autograph.

Years later, soon after I'd started my publicity business, I was walking through a MGM sound stage where they were shooting a picture called *The Venetian Affair*, and there was the original Frankenstein monster himself, Boris Karloff, sitting in his dressing room, deep in thought.

I had several encounters with John Carradine over the years, and after I started doing autograph shows in the late 1990s, I became acquainted with John Agar, who was really more associated with science-fiction movies (e.g. *Revenge of the Creature, Tarantula!*) than horror. In fact, I used to kid John with the question: "Who saved the world the most times, you or Richard Carlson?"[1]

He claimed it was Carlson, and I've never bothered to check to see if he was correct.

One afternoon during the late 1970s, I was on the 20th Century-Fox lot visiting a client, and who should I spot, but the Frankenstein monster, the Mummy and Dracula in person.

---

1. Carlson had starred in such sci-fi classics as *It Came From Outer Space* and *The Creature from the Black Lagoon*.

It was British horror star, Christopher Lee, who had appeared in many films for Hammer Pictures, but was certainly best known for his continuing portrayal as the sinister Count from Transylvania. Bela Lugosi may have originated the role of Dracula, but Lee's interpretation of the vampire king was much more powerful, frightening and sensual. No actor has ever equaled it.

I didn't meet Lee then, but a few days later, I was in the audience of the Pantages Theater in Hollywood, watching my client, Howard Keel, and his *Seven Brides for Seven Brothers* co-star, Jane Powell, in the opening night revival of the Tom Jones/Harvey Schmidt musical, *I Do! I Do!*

During intermission, I saw Lee in the lobby, and I approached him. I knew that he and Howard were friends, which gave me the perfect opening.[2] I introduced myself, told him that I would like to represent him, and we made a date to meet for lunch. Actually, Lee already knew who I was. He owned a copy of my book, *Basil Rathbone: His Life and His Films*.

Aside from his horror roles, Lee had also co-starred in movies like Richard Lester's *The Three Musketeers* (1973) and had played the lead villain in the James Bond adventure, *The Man With the Golden Gun* (1974). He had recently moved to Los Angeles with his wife and daughter in order to get better parts in important films, and had purchased a condominium apartment in a high rise building on Wilshire Boulevard between Beverly Hills and Westwood.

Christopher was a patrician, but down-to-earth, likable man, who insisted that he was an actor, *not* a horror film star. He was adamant about that, which became a minor problem selling him to the press, since the world knew him best as Count Dracula.[3]

He didn't help discourage that image much, since he continued to do movies in the horror/fantasy genre, and when he guest hosted on *Saturday Night Live*, he participated in a Dracula sketch.

He did, however, have a good sense of humor about his public per-

---

2. Several years earlier, when Howard was starring in a Los Angeles production of *Man of La Mancha* and before the Peter O'Toole movie had been cast, an interviewer asked him who he thought should star in the film version of the hit musical. His answer was "Christopher Lee." Truly, as I would learn later, Lee has a magnificent singing voice.

3. I had a similar problem when I briefly represented actress Christine Lahti while she was filming *Whose Life Is It Anyway?* (1981). Christine, who was not too well known at that time, is a tall lady, and she was not happy with the fact that much of the press that interviewed her wanted to know what it was like playing opposite short actors like Al Pacino and Richard Dreyfuss.

sona. I once quipped that, even though I was Jewish, I felt compelled to wear a Crucifix in his presence, which evoked a hearty laugh.

One story that Christopher enjoyed telling was about his first movie "role," a "spear carrier" in Laurence Olivier's Oscar-winning *Hamlet* (1948). Actually, Lee isn't even seen on-screen in the picture and, according to him, he wasn't paid anything. He happened to be at the studio that day for some reason and he snuck onto the *Hamlet* set. In the scene with the Players, when King Claudius gets upset and shouts, "Give me some light," several voices yell out "Lights!"

Among those unseen voices was Christopher Lee's, and that was his entire contribution to the film.

Christopher worked a lot of acting jobs during the year he was with me, including a role in Steven Spielberg's *1941*. At one point, he came to me and said that, although he was pleased with the press I had gotten for him, he didn't feel that he had a need for a personal publicist any longer, and we amicably parted ways. I don't know exactly when, but sometime after that, he moved back to England where he was knighted in 2009 and has continued to work steadily, including roles in quite a few horror (*Sleepy Hollow*), science-fiction (*Star Wars: Attack of the Clones*) and fantasy (*The Lord of the Rings*) films.

I guess you just can't keep a good horror star down.

While we're on the subject of fantasy characters: I also represented Spider-Man…sort of.

Nicholas Hammond, probably best remembered as playing "Friedrich," the eldest von Trapp son in the movie version of *The Sound of Music*, was a client of mine for about a year or more. He was cast as "Peter Parker/Spider-Man" in the short-lived 1977 television series, *The Amazing Spider-Man*; the first actor to play a live-action version of the superhero.

But, actually, he really only played Peter Parker. A stuntman did all the Spider-Man scenes. "I never put on the Spider-Man costume once," Nicholas confessed to me one day over lunch.

Abe Vigoda is not the only actor from *The Godfather* who, at one time or another, was my publicity client. I also represented Julie Gregg, the wife of "Sonny" (James Caan) in the picture, as well as Richard Castellano, who played the overweight "Clemenza" (*"Leave the gun. Take the cannoli."*). Richie had also received a Supporting Actor Oscar nomination for *Lovers and Other Strangers* (1970).

I really liked Richie, even if he was the "poster child" for angry actors.

I'm no shrink, so I'm not going to delve deep into the psychology of why people become actors or, for that matter, follow any artistic bent… like being a writer. Let's just say there was something missing from our childhoods, the feeling of being loved, perhaps, and let it go with that.

I don't think that anybody faces more rejection in their lives than actors. Sure, writers get plenty of rejections, but they come in an impersonal letter. ("*Thank you for letting us read your screenplay, however it does not fit our current needs.*")

With actors, it's more blunt.

Their agent, assuming they have one, submits them for a role in a movie, television show or stage play. They go to the casting office or the theater, where they find themselves waiting in a room filled with many other actors auditioning for the same role. When it's their turn to audition, they are ushered into another room or onto the stage where they face several people: the producer(s), the director, possibly the writer and the casting director, who are often talking on the phone, eating their lunch or chatting among themselves.

The poor actor is now supposed to put on a happy face in this atmosphere, and then convince these folks that he (or she) is the only person in the world that can play this role, which is quite often just a bit.

Chances are that, after reading just a few lines of the scene or singing a couple of bars from the song, one of the people will say, "Thank you very much. We'll let you know," and that is that. The actor has been dismissed, and he knows that he didn't get the part.

After enduring this kind of curt rejection time after time, is it any wonder that actors are angry people?

As a writer, director, sometimes co-producer and a former actor, I've been on both sides of the table, so I can commiserate with both the actor and the casting people.

When I was wearing one of my production hats, I always tried to make the actors feel good about their audition, even if I knew that I wasn't going to cast them. Often, after they read through the scene once, I would give them a bit of direction, simply to see if they could incorporate that direction into a second reading of the scene.

I tried to treat these artists who were, figuratively, "standing naked" in front of me, like people.

One thing that an actor should remember: If you don't get a particular role, it's not necessarily because you are not a talented actor. If you didn't have talent, you probably wouldn't have been allowed to audition in the first place.

More likely, you did not fit the writer and/or director's conception of the character. There have been situations where I did not cast the better actor simply because he did not match my vision of the role being cast. True, there have times when an actor delivered a knockout audition that made me adjust my conception and I wound up casting him, but those instances have been few and far between.

As previously stated, Richard Castellano was definitely an angry actor, and his primary enemy was anybody who bore the title, "Producer." He would often relate the tale of how, at one stage audition early in his career, the casting person sitting in the dark auditorium had dismissed him before he'd read a single line. When Richie objected to this person he could not even see, the guy said something like, "Go, or you'll never work in this town again."

"Who do you think you are?" Richie retorted loudly. "How dare you try to prevent me from following my chosen profession."

I believe he had to be escorted from the theater that day.

Castellano became my client in the spring of 1972, around the time *The Godfather* was released. The actor, whose home was in New Jersey, had come to Los Angeles to star in a summer television series, *The Super*.

I don't really remember how he happened to choose me to be his publicist. I guess somebody recommended me. I got a call from Castellano's manager to come meet with his client. Richie and I hit it off, and that was that.

With the recent Oscar nomination and *The Godfather* under his belt, Castellano was "hot," and the problem was that he knew it. He started throwing his weight around, both literally and figuratively, making demands, often unreasonable, to the producers of his series, who tried to comply in order to keep their star happy.

He would never admit it, and perhaps he didn't even realize it, but Richie was getting his revenge for all the slights he'd suffered when he was an unknown actor.

Castellano demanded that his daughter, Margaret, be cast as his daughter on the series and that his "writing partner," Ardell Sheridan, play his wife.[4] Both Margaret, nicknamed "Mouse," and Ardell may have

---

4. Several years later, Castellano would divorce his wife of many years and marry Sheridan.

been nice people and I liked them both, but their professional acting experience at that time was definitely limited. Nevertheless, if the producers wanted Richie, these ladies were part of the package.

Bruno Kirby, who would play the young "Clemenza," in *The Godfather, Part II*, was cast in the role of Castellano's son.

If the show's producers thought that acquiescing to Castellano's casting demands would pacify him, they were mistaken. Richie apparently wanted artistic control over the entire series.

My friend, actor/writer/director Bruce Kimmel, who was cast in an episode of the series, recalls going to the first table read of the show: "Castellano walks into the room with his entourage, and in front of Rob Reiner and Phil Mishkin, the series' creators, tosses the script down onto the ground, stomps on it, and shouts, 'This is shit!'"

The Super was not a good show, and was cancelled after ten episodes.

The timeline with Riche over the next two or three years is a bit vague in my memory. I do recall that while I was still married to Terry, he and his family came to our home in Agoura Hills one Christmas where my son, David, who was about four then, had fun "shooting" him with a toy gun he'd received as a present. [*Richie "died" beautifully.*] I also recollect that when I visited New York City for the first time (1973), he picked me up at my hotel and drove me out to New Jersey where we met with Ardell in her apartment. He had lost a lot of weight then, and looked healthy.

Work-wise, he'd done a couple of television movies after *The Super* in which he'd played a mobster, and he'd also *not* been cast in *The Godfather, Part II*. Different people have different explanations as to why he wasn't in that picture. I don't know the real reason and I'm not going to speculate. All I'm going to say is: "Richie, wherever you might be, you made a big mistake not doing that movie."

Castellano's war with producers would continue. In 1975, I represented him again when he was offered another television series, *Joe & Sons*. Since he hadn't worked for a while, he didn't have casting approval on that one, but he continued to give the producers a difficult time.

Castellano had come from a Sicilian background and he claimed that, although he was not a part of it, he had Mob connections. Francis Ford Coppola had, in fact, used him as somewhat of a technical consultant during the filming of *The Godfather*.

Producers in Hollywood were a bit frightened of him. Although I never witnessed it myself, it's my understanding that he would often make veiled threats against these creative people in order to get what he demanded.

Joe & Sons was cancelled after fourteen episodes, and Richie seldom worked in films or television after that. He died of a heart attack in 1988.

Richard Castellano was a talented man who could have had a major, ongoing career as a character actor…if only he'd learned to "play nice".

If Richard Castellano was the angriest client I ever represented, then Charles Nelson Reilly was definitely one of the most unusual.

Most people remember Reilly for his appearances on *Match Game* or other television variety and game shows, but before that he was a Tony Award-winning actor who originated major roles in such Broadway hits as *How to Succeed in Business Without Really Trying* and *Hello, Dolly!*.

I met Charles in 1968 after he had moved out to the West Coast and was co-starring in the weekly television series, *The Ghost and Mrs. Muir* with Hope Lange and Edward Mulhare. My entrée to him was my friend and client, Stanley Rubin, who was producing the series for 20th Century-Fox.[5]

There's no question that Charles was an extremely talented and dedicated actor, comedian and director, but he was also somewhat scatterbrained when it came to the real world. Indeed, at least in his dealings with me, I found him to be not unlike his public persona.

He might have been frustrating to deal with on a practical level, but you could not *not* like Charles. He had a good heart…and he was funny to be around.

He was also quite friendly toward me, perhaps a bit *too* friendly.

Whenever we met at a restaurant or were doing an interview with a member of the press, I always tried to sit across the table from Charles. I'd learned that, if I sat next to him, his hand would inevitably find its way to my leg.

I don't believe that there was anything sexual in what he did. He knew that I was straight. I think he was just nervous and that the action was really involuntary…but it did make me feel a bit uncomfortable.

While he was my client, Charles became a semi-regular on *The Dean Martin Show*. It was well known in the show business community that the popular host of the weekly variety program attended few, if any, rehearsals and that both he and most of his guests read their dialogue off of cue cards.

---

5. I spent a lot of time at Fox during the late 1960s. Not only did I represent Charles Nelson Reilly, but I also worked with Karen Jensen and Madlyn Rhue, who were on *Bracken's World*, another Stanley Rubin-produced series, and Deanna Lund from the *Land of the Giants* series. Later, in 1974, Mark Lenard became a client while he was co-starring on the *Planet of the Apes* television series with Roddy McDowall.

Charles, initially, found this practice to be appalling. He was a serious actor, trained in the theatre, and he knew that an actor's first responsibility was to learn his lines.

However, working in Hollywood and, in particular, on television variety shows, even the most dedicated performer can forget their origins.

One afternoon, Charles was driving his convertible, top down, to the NBC Studio where *The Dean Martin Show* was taped, when a strong gust of wind came along, blowing his script for that week out of the car. Pages scattered everywhere down the canyon.

His first instinct was to stop the car, and go retrieve the pages. Then, he said to himself, "What the hell! This is Hollywood. I'll just read it off the cue cards." And, that's the way he did television variety shows from then on.

Charles was a "hot" property when I represented him. Virtually every talk and variety show, national and local, wanted to book him because he was a fun guest.

His popularity made my job easy, but it also created a problem, which Charles didn't seem to appreciate, or if he did, he chose to ignore. That became incredibly frustrating.

When you have a "hot" client, the smart agent or publicist picks and chooses the gigs that he accepts for that client. If it's a well-paying job, like a movie or network variety show, that's one thing, but talk shows pay virtually nothing and local shows of any kind pay even less. What you want to protect your client from is overexposure, because once that happens; he will cool off pretty quickly.

Charles listened when I told him that, then he would go ahead and book himself on talk show after talk show, even the most insignificant ones. I'm not suggesting that this overexposure killed his career…because it didn't. However, I do believe that, after *The Ghost and Mrs. Muir* and *The Dean Martin Show* left the air, Reilly found that his options were limited to being more of a "personality" than an actor, which is part of the reason why he transitioned into becoming a stage director…and a successful one.

The final straw that ended my professional relationship with Charles was when I booked him to ride in the Thanksgiving Parade down Hollywood Boulevard, a prestigious event. I was planning to watch the parade on television when, about fifteen minutes before it was to start, Charles called me, and said: "I've decided that I don't want to do this," then he hung up.

There was nobody that I could call at that late time, so the procession proceeded without Charles Nelson Reilly. But, there was an empty convertible bearing a banner with his name as part of the parade.

I encountered Charles in a Sunset Strip bookstore several years later. "Oh yes," he said, "You're the publicist." We had a short, pleasant conversation. The one thing that struck me is that he was much more subdued than when I had known him previously.

That's Dad, Mom and cute little me.

The house where we lived until I was eleven years old:
1239 23rd North (*now 23rd East*).

Our summer home at Lake Lucerne. That's my folks and me on the dock, my grandmother and cousin, Sandra, in the rowboat, and my aunt, Lee, sitting on the wall. I'm not sure if this place reminds me of *On Golden Pond* or Crystal Lake from the *Friday the 13th* movies.

During World War II, my father had no problem using my image to advertise his jewelry store. I know the ad is very patriotic, but I was "the talent," and all I ever got out of this deal was an ice cream cone.

Here's the whole family, including our dog, Lucy, at the summer home in Soap Lake, WA. The people on the right, avoiding the camera, are friends of my folks, visiting from Seattle.

Seattle's mayor, Alan Pomeroy, congratulates me on my bar mitzvah.

Photo Section • 83

My Garfield High School Senior Play, *A Slight Case of Murder*: Jenny Maxwell, Paul Offenhenden, Linda Scheel and me. I'm wearing my father's Edward G. Robinson (*Little Caesar*) vest.

Mrs. Patricia Borgstrom, my high school drama teacher, who believed in my abilities. This photo was taken in 2004 at my 45th high school reunion.

During my freshman year at the University of Washington Drama Department, I played "Grumio" in *The Taming of the Shrew* with Michael Pierce and my dear friend, Marian Hailey.

My character was smitten with "mermaid" Yoland Johnson in the UW production of *Miranda*. (University of Washington, Special Collections, UW 33533.)

That's me (in front with the clipboard) with the cast of the one act play I directed for the nurses' group. I apologize, but there was no program and I do not remember the names of any of these other people.

Here I am: producer, director and star of *Blue Denim*. Big mistake!

My first *paid* gig ($10 and a box lunch): I was an extra in *It Happened at the World's Fair*. That's Kurt Russell, me (facing left) and Elvis. If you're wondering why the photo is a bit distorted, it's because it's actually a frame from the 35mm film without benefit of the widescreen lens. On the day the movie opened at Seattle's Orpheum Theater, I talked the projectionist into cutting that frame out of the theater's print and giving it to me. *Wasn't I resourceful?*

Ann Gray and me at a college dance. She's the one that got away, but we are still "buddies".

That's future wife Terry and me in *The Grass Is Greener*, the last time I ever acted on stage. I kind of like the mustache. Don't you?

This is the Actor's Theatre production of *Suddenly Last Summer*. That's Terry, on her knees, doing the Elizabeth Taylor role. Also, from left: Vern D. Wheeler, Sheila Falkner, Charlotte Cotter, Gene Marshall, Marian Hopkins (fantastic actress) and Beverly Welsh.

A newspaper clipping promoting the Chapel Theatre production of *A Thousand Clowns* that I directed. I'm with Fred Ward and Merrell-Ann Haddan.

FINAL REHEARSALS are taking place at the Chapel Theater, Torrance for Friday's opening of "a Thousand Clowns." Director Michael Druxman (right) explains a scene to Fred West and Merrell Haddan.

Gigi Perreau was supposed to play the female lead in *Journey From a Desolate Place*, my film that never got made. We've never actually worked together, but this delightful lady surprised me when she suddenly appeared at my 2010 book signing for *My Forty-Five Years in Hollywood...And How I Escaped Alive*.

Client Reed Hadley had one of those voices that you never forget.

My client, James Griffith, had a face you knew, but the name escaped you.

Don Keefer was a client who got to wear a pointed hat in this memorable episode of *The Twilight Zone*.

Eccentric client Aram Katcher caused a few problems when he played Napoleon Bonaparte in an episode of *I Dream of Jeannie* with Barbara Eden.

Debi Storm was one of my first publicity clients. She was five or six years old back then, and appearing in a movie with Bob Hope. We reconnected a few years ago when we were both appearing at a Hollywood autograph show.

Diane McBain was a longtime publicity client and remains a good friend.

As a publicist, I had the opportunity to visit a lot of interesting places, like the Wright Brothers monument in Nags Head, NC.

On one of my publicity jaunts, Steve Kanaly, actress Susan Sullivan (*Falcon Crest*) and I were given a private tour of The White House…

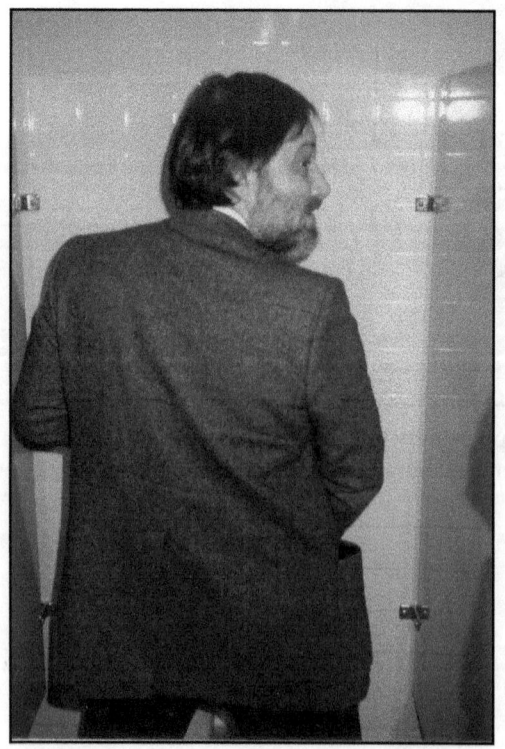

…where I left a memento in the men's room.

Here I am with my late former father-in-law, comedy writer Ray Singer, client and friend Henry Darrow and his lovely wife, Lauren.

My friend, Ed Siemens, built his own sailboat.
Here I am at the wheel, looking very macho.
Actually, I was very seasick.

With Michael and Beverly Ansara. By this time in his career, Michael had adopted his Yul Brynner look.

With actor/client George Dickerson and his beautiful wife, Suzanne. The Dickersons reside in a Greenwich Village apartment, haunted by the ghost of writer James Agee.

12

Jane Fonda, George Raft & Other Non-Clients

ALTHOUGH, I'VE NEVER AGREED with her politics, I've always admired Jane Fonda as a fine, intelligent actress. *Klute, Julia, Coming Home, California Suite, The China Syndrome* and *On Golden Pond* are superb, entertaining films that I can watch time and time again, despite any biased message they might contain.

I have never actually met Ms. Fonda, but I have been present to witness a few minor, albeit interesting, moments in her career.

In 1969, at the height of the Vietnam War protests, of which Jane Fonda was a viable part, a new television game show began in Hollywood. It was called *The Movie Game*, and, as you might expect, all of the questions contestants answered had to do with movies, past and present. Teams, made up of two celebrities and one "civilian" contestant, would play against each other for the "grand prize," whatever that was.

And, wouldn't you know it, but the civilians always knew many more of the answers than their celebrity teammates did.

Being a movie buff, I even tried out to be a contestant, but I wasn't chosen, most likely because the host of the show was *Variety* columnist Army Archerd who, as a publicist, I worked with on a daily basis. Had I become a contestant that would definitely have raised some questions about the integrity of the show.

Probably because they were friends with Army Archerd, virtually every star in town would, sooner or later, appear on *The Movie Game*. People like John Wayne, Vincent Price, David Janssen and George Peppard are just a few of the names who took part in both answering questions and performing a clue-filled sketch on the half-hour, five days per week, show.

As is the case with most television game shows, *The Movie Game* taped a week's worth of shows in one afternoon. For one of these five show marathons, I accompanied client Jack Carter to the studio and sat with him in the green room. Edmond O'Brien was another celebrity contestant that day, as was Jane Fonda, who didn't appear pleased to be there. Indeed, once the first of the five shows started taping, I seem to recall that she tried to inject some political comments into the proceedings, but she was cut off by Archerd, who politely reminded her that this was an entertainment game show, not a talk show.

Later, when it came time for her to participate in the sketch, she complained, saying something like, "Oh, do I have to perform in that stupid thing?"

Upon which Army commented, "Last week, we had an actor on the show named 'Henry Fonda'. He performed in that 'stupid thing' and he enjoyed it."

I had to leave for a meeting after the first show finished taping, but Carter later informed me that, following the taping of the second show, Jane Fonda either asked or *was asked* to leave. He wasn't sure which.

I believe that Connie Stevens, who was visiting elsewhere on the studio lot that day, replaced her on the final three shows.

This next story isn't really about Ms. Fonda, but she was present.

Not too long after I started representing him, I'd booked my client, Michael Ansara, on a local one-hour, roundtable talk show that discussed serious topics of the day. Fonda was one of the other guests, as was comedian Morey Amsterdam.

Michael, as I would soon learn, was not a good match for this kind of a program. In a one-on-one interview, he would do fine, but in this kind of situation with several other people talking; he was more apt to just sit and listen, rather than to inject himself into the conversation.

About halfway through the show, the discussion was going fine. Fonda was talking about her political views. Amsterdam was making quips, and the host and other guests were contributing to the dialogue. Michael, however, had yet to say a word.

Finally, the host of the show turned to Michael and asked him a direct question. Michael started to answer, but Amsterdam interrupted him with, "I'm so glad to be here at the opening of your mouth."

Michael chuckled, and then answered the question.

Amsterdam, incidentally was a close friend of my late former father-in-law, comedy writer Ray Singer. In fact, Morey shot the videos at the reception of my wedding to Ray's daughter, Laurie…a union that lasted all of ten months.

The comedian told me that he had known every President since Roosevelt, and the only one that he didn't like was Jimmy Carter. "He reminded me of a ventriloquist's dummy," he said.

In 1977, Jane Fonda won the Golden Apple Award, presented by the Hollywood Women's Press Club. I attended that Sunday afternoon luncheon in Beverly Hills.

The presenter of that prize was John Wayne, politically the complete polar opposite of Fonda. When she walked up onto the stage and stood next to Wayne, the audience laughed and applauded at the irony of the situation, as did Fonda who appeared to have "lightened up" during the past few years.

Finally, Wayne quipped, "I'm so glad that you're standing to my right," which, of course, broke up the house again.

Val de Vargas was an actor that I represented for a year or two. You may or may not recognize the name, but he did work in many films and television shows from the 1950s on. He's quite prominent in movies like *Touch of Evil*, *The Magnificent Seven*, *Hatari!* and *Hellfighters*. When he wasn't acting, Val did well as a real estate broker.

Val and his then-wife used to throw an annual Christmas party in their Hollywood Hills home, and on two consecutive years during the mid-1970s, I attended those gatherings with Terry, to whom I was still married. Also in attendance on both occasions was actress Rosemary Forsyth (*Shenandoah*, *The War Lord*).

At the first of these two parties, Rosemary was there with her then husband, Ron Waranch, who I chatted with and he seemed to be a nice guy. I also talked a bit to Rosemary. She was also nice, but she did appear to have had a few too many drinks.

Minutes later, Terry, who also had had a couple of drinks, *complimented* Rosemary on her dress…but that's not what Rosemary apparently heard. With the alcohol in her system, she thought that Terry had insulted her, and she snarled something nasty back at her.

Terry was not the kind of person to quietly accept an insult, particularly after she had been drinking, so she started to retort. Not wanting to get between two angry women who might start pulling each other's hair out, I took Terry firmly by the arm and whispered, "Just stop it. Let it go."

She got the message. Rosemary's husband moved her out of the room, and that was that.

Fast forward to a year later and the next de Vargas Christmas party. I'm there with Terry, and who should walk in, but Rosemary Forsyth... without her husband.

Appearing quite sober, she walked over to us and, I believe, also to everybody else at the party and said, "If I was rude or insulted you last year, I humbly apologize."

I have always been a big fan of gangster movies. As I mentioned earlier, many films of Humphrey Bogart, James Cagney, Edward G. Robinson, George Raft and Broderick Crawford are at the top of the list as my all-time favorites.

I never had the opportunity to meet either Bogart or Cagney, but I did spend an enjoyable few minutes chatting with Robinson at an afternoon party at Edd Byrnes' house, and I also got to know both Raft and Crawford.

George Raft, one of Hollywood's biggest stars during the 1930s and 40s, freely admitted that he was no actor. What he did possess was a powerful screen presence, particularly in sinister and "tough guy" roles. The original *Scarface* (1932) with Paul Muni, *Souls at Sea* (1937) with Gary Cooper, *Each Dawn I Die* (1939) with James Cagney and *They Drive By Night* (1940) co-starring Ann Sheridan, Ida Lupino and Humphrey Bogart probably contain his most impressive screen moments, but younger audiences will remember him best in Billy Wilder's *Some Like It Hot* with Marilyn Monroe, Tony Curtis and Jack Lemmon.

If any actor sabotaged his own career, it was George Raft. For various seemingly implausible reasons, he refused do films like *Dead End*, *High Sierra*, *The Maltese Falcon* and even, as has been rumored, *Casablanca*. All of these refused roles wound up being played by a then "B" picture player, Humphrey Bogart, and they made him the biggest star in Hollywood.

As I quickly ascertained when I lunched with Raft at the Beverly Hills Brown Derby, he may have been a nice and likable man, but he was definitely not the sharpest knife in the drawer.

He told me about an experience he had had somewhat recently, working for director Otto Preminger on a film called *Skidoo*. As it turned out, the picture was a major turkey, but it did have a top cast, headed by Jackie Gleason, thus while it was in production, it was considered to be an "A" project in Hollywood. More significantly for Raft, who had had big problems with the IRS and, it's said, was living on handouts from friends like Frank Sinatra, this was the first "important" movie he'd been in for many years, so perhaps he should have been a bit grateful to Preminger.

Instead, while they were shooting a scene one afternoon that appeared to be running late, Raft confronted the director with: "You told me that we would finish this scene in time for me to get home and watch the baseball game on television."

Holding his well-known Prussian temper in check, Preminger explained to the actor that there had been technical delays that he could not foresee, and that he would finish with him as soon as possible. But, Raft would have none of that. He told the director that if his scene wasn't completed in an hour, he would go home anyway.

How to win friends and influence people, right?

Jack Warner, who had the actor under contract to his studio for a few years, told an even better story about Raft's lack of acumen.

Both men were unhappy with the arrangement. Raft had been turning down almost every role presented to him and a frustrated Warner, who was personally fond of the actor, wanted to buy out the rest of his contract. "How about ten thousand dollars?" Warner proposed as settlement that day in his office.

"That sounds fair," Raft said, then proceeded to write out a check for that amount.

Warner recalled that he couldn't believe what was happening, but as soon as Raft left his office, he ran to the bank to cash the check.

I have nothing but warm memories about Raft. After our lunch at the Brown Derby, we would talk every so often, and he always was gracious about giving me anecdotes that I could use in my books, particularly *Paul Muni: His Life and His Films.*

Truthfully, I felt sorry for the man. He may have dug his own grave, so to speak, in Hollywood, but it was still depressing to see this once major star having to act as a "host" in a fine Beverly Hills restaurant, moving from table-to-table, chatting with the customers, probably in return for a free meal and a few dollars in his pocket.

That's what he was doing the last time I saw him. I was there for dinner with Jack Carter, singer Fran Jeffries and her then-husband, director Richard Quine.

Raft never came over to our table. Perhaps he was too embarrassed.

Broderick Crawford may have won the Academy Award for *All the King's Men* (1949), yet his stardom never really ascended to the same heights as that of Bogart, Cagney, Robinson or even Raft. Nevertheless, he was a favorite actor of mine during my high school years. I relished his beefy tough guy roles, his snappy delivery of dialogue in films like *Born Yesterday*, *The Mob*, *Scandal Sheet*, *Human Desire* and the little known, but excellent Western, *The Last Posse*. He also starred with Claire Trevor in *Stop, You're Killing Me*, a 1952 musical remake of *A Slight Case of Murder*, which, as you will recall, had been my high school senior play.

Following the cancellation of his hit syndicated series, *Highway Patrol*; Crawford's career had not gone well. Most of his work had been as a guest star on episodic television or playing cameo roles in forgettable theatrical features (e.g. *Up From the Beach*, *The Oscar*).

I decided that I wanted to be his publicist. After all, who could do a better job for him than a true fan?

Somehow or another, I got his phone number and we made a date to meet at the Hollywood Brown Derby for lunch.[1]

Crawford was a soft-spoken gentleman whose walk reminded me of John Wayne's, the result, he said, of a long ago hip injury. The meeting went well. We had a good rapport, but he didn't hire me. I don't recall the rationale he gave for turning me down, but I think the real reason was that he was hurting financially. As I would discover shortly, he was living in an inexpensive Hollywood motel on Vine Street near Melrose Boulevard.

Brod and I would talk every now and then on the phone, and it was always a friendly conversation. Then, in 1970, he was cast as one of the leads in a new television series, *The Interns*, filmed at the Columbia Studios on Gower Street. One of the actors on that show, incidentally, was Mike Farrell, who I'd turned down years before as a publicity client.

When my friend and client, Bridget Hanley, guest starred on that series, I visited her on the set. Brod welcomed me and invited me to sit

---

1. Often I would cold call an older, former star at home to see if I could sell them on becoming a publicity client. Successful or not, those conversations could be quite interesting...and revealing. Dana Andrews (*Laura*, *The Best Years of Our Lives*), for example, confessed that: "I don't think you can help me, Michael. I'm a drunkard, and the studios won't hire me any more." *Hmm*...I wonder what he would have told me if I wasn't a total stranger.

with him in his dressing room. We had a nice talk, but I could tell that he'd been drinking.

The Interns was not picked up for a second season, however before that announcement was made, word had leaked out in the trade papers that, *had* the show gone into a sophomore year, the plan was to replace Crawford with actor Lew Ayres. No reason was given, but I assumed that Brod's well-known penchant for alcohol was a contributing factor.

Recently, however, I met and was interviewed by a writer from Chicago, Ralph Schiller, who is researching a full biography of Crawford, and he told me something rather interesting. Brod's problems near the end of his career might not have been caused by alcohol issues, but by his fear that he was going blind. According to Schiller, who was still trying to get verification of those facts, the actor felt that he could still find work… even if producers thought that he had a drinking problem…but not if he lost his sight.

I thought about what Schiller said, then remembered that Brod's eyes were small and narrow, like he was always straining to see you. I also recalled his appearance on *Saturday Night Live* in 1997. As the guest host, he had surprisingly little to do on the ninety-minute variety show, and in one spoof of his *Highway Patrol* series; he spent most of his time leaning against a car.

Alcohol or eyesight? It could have been a result of either one.

When I heard that Brod was a patient at the Motion Picture Country Home, I wanted to visit him, but I was advised that that was not a good idea. He didn't want visitors, so I respected that. He passed away in 1986.

I was introduced to John Houseman in 1980 at a Sunday afternoon party at the home of my friend and client, Dan O'Herlihy. He and Dan had a long history together, both having worked extensively with Orson Welles.

Houseman, who had won an Oscar for playing the no-nonsense "Professor Kingsfield" in *The Paper Chase*, was quite genial, not a bit like the stern-face Harvard law professor, which he was currently reprising in a television series of the same name.

At one point, we were seated at a table, along with a woman who wrote movie reviews for the *Los Angeles Times*. She had recently given a negative assessment to director Walter Hill's *The Long Riders*, a revisionist Western, which I had liked. Along with David Carradine, Stacy Keach, Dennis Quaid and others, it had also starred my then-client, James Keach, as the infamous outlaw, Jesse James.

"What did you like about it?" she asked me.

I told her that, aside from the fact that I thought it was well acted and had a nice gritty style to it, the picture gave an interesting and fresh look at historical events that had been dramatized many times before on film. As I continued, I happened to glance over at Houseman, who was listening to my assessment.

But, it wasn't John Houseman sitting there watching me. The person I saw was "Professor Kingsfield," and he was giving me that unyielding stare that made me feel that I should have studied the day's lesson a bit better.

It was, to say the least, a disconcerting moment.

One afternoon in the late 1960s, the owner of an upscale coffee shop in Brentwood asked me to come by and talk to him about my possibly publicizing his restaurant. When I got there, he was busy with another matter, so he introduced me to one of his favorite customers, and she invited me to sit with her and her son until he was free,

The lady was actress Anna Kashfi, who had played prominent roles in films like *The Mountain* with Spencer Tracy and *Battle Hymn* with Rock Hudson, but was certainly best known as being the first wife of Marlon Brando, and the mother of his son, Christian.

I spent perhaps fifteen or twenty minutes chatting with the pleasant Ms. Kashfi about this and that. My impression of Christian, who appeared to be about eleven at the time, was that he was a quiet, well-mannered young man.

In 1990, this same quiet, well-mannered young man shot and killed his half-sister's boy friend in his father's Los Angeles home. He pled guilty to manslaughter, and served five years in prison.

One never knows what the future holds.

My first book, *Paul Muni: His Life and His Films*, was published in 1974, and that summer I flew up to Seattle with my son, David, to promote the book and also visit family.

Diane, my attractive, soon to be former sister-in-law, chauffeured me around to my various publicity appointments, and one morning we were sitting in the green room of KING-TV, as I waited to be interviewed on the local "Good Morning" show. Also waiting to be interviewed was Oscar-winner Gig Young (*They Shoot Horses, Don't They?*), who was in town performing in a stage production of *Harvey*.

Young looked dissipated, probably from his years of alcohol abuse, but he still had that mischievous twinkle in his eye that made him so likable on screen. The one thing I do remember from our genial conversation that day was that he kept insisting that Diane must be my girl friend and not my sister-in-law.

A few years later, the troubled actor would murder his new wife, and then blow his own brains out in his New York apartment.

Christian Brando…Gig Young….Makes me wonder if I'm a jinx.

When Howard Keel was preparing to do *I Do! I Do!*, he expressed an interest in seeing the 1952 movie of *The Four Poster* with Rex Harrison and Lilli Palmer, which was adapted from the Jan de Hartog stage play. The two-person play was the basis for the hit musical that had starred Mary Martin and Robert Preston on Broadway. I was fortunate to have seen them reprise their roles when the show had played in downtown Los Angeles.

I called some people I knew at Columbia Pictures, and they were kind enough to arrange a screening for Howard at the studio. Since I'd never seen the movie, I also attended.

At that screening, Howard introduced me to a friend, actor Jon Cypher, who had not only played "Prince Charming" opposite Julie Andrews in the 1957 television production of Rodgers and Hammerstein's *Cinderella*, but had also been the lead heavy in a good, but not well known, Burt Lancaster Western, *Valdez Is Coming* (1971).

It might have been a year or two later that Terry and I were having major problems. We went to a marriage counselor and, at one of our sessions; he asked if his new intern could sit in. We had no objection, so he called the person into the room.

It was Jon Cypher. Apparently, his acting career was not going well and he was preparing to switch professions.

Jon sat in on the next few sessions, but it soon became obvious that Terry and I were never going to have a meeting of the minds. We terminated the therapy and, eventually, divorced.

I think it must have been within a year after that that I attended a performance of *Evita* at the Shubert Theater in Los Angeles. And, who was playing "Peron" in that production?

That's right. Jon Cypher.

Jon would go on to guest star and play running roles on many television series, but is probably best remembered as "Chief Fletcher Daniels" on *Hill Street Blues*.

Why did I tell you this story?

Because Jon Cypher is the perfect illustration of *TENACITY*. He is proof-positive why an artist, be he/she an actor, writer, director or whatever, should never give up his/her dream. You might have a lot of dark, depressing times in your career, but you never know when that one special break is going to come your way.

13

Michael Ansara

I FIRST MET MICHAEL ANSARA IN 1969. He was married to Barbara Eden then, the star of the hit television series, *I Dream of Jeannie*. He just called me out of the blue to talk about possible press representation for both him and his wife.

After starring in two successful television series, *Broken Arrow* (as Apache chief "Cochise") and *Law of the Plainsman*, during the late 1950s and early 1960s, Michael was one of the busiest character actors in Hollywood, a regular guest star on television and a prominent supporting player in movies (e.g. *Voyage to the Bottom of the Sea*, *The Comancheros*). His roots were Lebanese, yet he was often cast as a Native American, Mexican, Arab or member of another non-WASP group. He was, in fact, the first actor to play a "Klingon" on the *Star Trek* series, a role that he would reprise on that show's various offshoots.

We met at a Sunset Strip restaurant where he insisted on picking up the check, since he was not going to hire me then. He was about to leave for Spain where he was going to play the lead heavy in *Guns of the Magnificent Seven*, the third film in the popular Western franchise, which would star George Kennedy in the role originated by Yul Brynner.

Had it not been for Barbara, I think that Michael would have hired me right after he returned from Spain a few weeks later, but they had recently signed with a new manager, who was also a publicist, and Barbara was comfortable in that situation.

I pursued Michael for the better part of a year, phoning him every two months or so to see if his and Barbara's circumstances had changed. They hadn't for her, but I could sense that, as far as his career was concerned, he was not happy with this manager with whom he'd also signed.

Finally, I suggested that he let Barbara stay with the manager, but that he let me represent him…and he agreed.

I don't know if Michael initially signed with me just because I kept bugging him, but if that's true, I'm fine with that.

Once again, TENACITY is the key to success in show business or any other business.

Charles Champlin, the long time, respected motion picture editor and chief critic at the *Los Angeles Times*, once confessed that he'd at long last agreed to interview one of my clients "just to get rid of me." I'd been after him to do a piece on this actor for three years.

Also, as you read in the Preface of this book, I've never made it a secret that it took me ten years of trying before I sold my first screenplay.

English biologist and Darwinian Thomas Huxley once said: "Patience and tenacity are worth more than twice their weight of cleverness."

Almost immediately, Michael and I became best of friends. We spoke almost daily, lunched together often and I made sure that his name was in the trade papers on a regular basis. Michael and Barbara, a warm and gracious hostess, welcomed me into their Sherman Oaks home and I spent a lot of time there. I also became friendly with their son, Matthew, a year or two older than my son, David, and every now and then I would bring David with me when I visited the Ansaras, so that the boys could play together while Michael and I talked business.

Work wise, Michael guest starred frequently on episodic television and movies, as well as occasionally doing roles in theatrical features. *I even got him a part in The Doll Squad*, a film directed by Ted V. Mikels, my cameraman/editor for *Genesis*. Best known for schlock horror films like *The Astro Zombies*, *The Corpse Grinders* and *Blood Orgy of the She-Devils*, Ted was attempting to upgrade the quality of movies he was making with this ultra low budget female action movie, a precursor to *Charlie's Angels*.

Michael only worked two days on *The Doll Squad* (1973), much of which was shot at Zsa Zsa Gabor's home. Despite the fact that I did get him top billing and an excellent salary for that time ($1000 per day), I'm not sure he has ever totally forgiven me for putting him into that turkey.

On the other hand, in the movie business, a paying job is a paying job, and as my mentor, producer Stanley Rubin, once told me: "If a movie is bad, nobody important is going to see it anyway."

When Michael celebrated his eightieth birthday, I couldn't help but have some fun with him. The present I gave him was a DVD of *The Doll Squad*.

Michael had directed an episode of *I Dream of Jeannie*, and he was interested in doing more directing assignments. My dream, of course, was to write for and make movies, so we put our heads together to see if we could get a film project off the ground.

Keeping in mind that we would be working with a miniscule budget, I wrote a screenplay, entitled *Death of a Moroon*.[1] The story structure was borrowed from Victor Hugo's *The Hunchback of Notre Dame*, but John Steinbeck's *Of Mice and Men* influenced the characters. The idea was that I would produce the picture and Michael would direct.

Having worked with Ted Mikels, I knew that we could shoot this film (non-union) in three weeks for a budget of well under $200,000 with one or two non-star "names". Indeed, at one point, Warren Oates was suggested for a role, and I even approached Richard Castellano about doing one of the leads as a personal favor.

Actually, Richie agreed to do it, but then, since I was now wearing a producer's hat, he forgot that we were "friends," and started making unreasonable demands, so I stopped talking to him about it and moved on.

Michael and I may have had great enthusiasm for *Death of a Moroon*, but enthusiasm will only take you so far. Before we could move forward, we had to come up with the financing.

I met a personal manager, who said that she could get us the money…with one caveat: If she succeeded, her client…an unknown and fairly inexperienced actress… would play the leading role.

Honestly, I do not recall the names of these people, so we'll call the manager "Edith" and the actress "Sophie".

We auditioned Sophie, and although she wasn't a bad actress, neither Michael nor I really wanted to use her. Michael was concerned that, since we were on such a short filming schedule, he would not have sufficient time to draw out of her the performance that was required for what was, dramatically, the most complex role in the picture. And, as the producer, I would have preferred to have an actress with some sort of name value.

---

1. When I was a kid in Soap Lake, Washington, I heard "The Storyman" mispronounce the word "moron" as "moroon". That mispronunciation worked for me in this script.

On the other hand, *if* Edith could get us the money, we were really not in a strong bargaining position, so we reluctantly agreed. However, we had a plan that, if it succeeded, would let us have our cake and eat it, too.

This was the early 1970s and, with the Motion Picture Production Code recently abandoned, nudity abounded in movies. Today, naked folks, even on television, are no big deal, but back then, seeing major stars on screen in the buff sold a lot of tickets. As Roger Corman would tell me years later: "Nudity is the cheapest special effect you can have in a movie."

Over the years, people (all guys) have expressed envy at the fact that I have worked with beautiful actresses who performed nude, and I must admit that, like any other red-blooded male, the "idea" of seeing some of these ladies in the buff certainly had its appeal. But, the reality is that, when you are actually doing these scenes, the people behind the camera are just as uncomfortable as the people performing in front of it, and you want to finish them up just as soon as possible.

That said, there was a key scene in *Death of a Moroon* that would require full frontal nudity from Sophie, and she was protesting doing that. Edith's position was more middle-of-the-road. She realized that the scene was necessary to the story, so she assured us that, if her client backed out of the project that would not stop her from brokering a deal with her money people.

Edith's investors were from the Midwest, and during this period, their representative flew into Los Angeles for a meeting with Michael and me. That sit down went okay, but at one point, I wished that Michael had not been present.

As I said in an earlier chapter, Michael Ansara is one of the most honest and honorable people that I have ever known, but when you are doing business, sometimes being *too* honest can be a handicap.

Don't misunderstand. I also consider myself to be an honest and honorable person. I abhor lying. I abhor cheating. And, I believe in full disclosure. However, when you are in a business meeting and trying to sell something, in this case our motion picture to investors, if you don't know the answer, you keep your mouth shut and defer to the people who do know.

Michael was an intelligent man, but his experience in the business world was little or none. As an actor, he had worked in film and television shows that were budgeted for millions of dollars, and he never had to be concerned with planning shooting schedules or other practicalities. All he had to be concerned with was knowing his lines, hitting his mark and giving a good performance. Even when he directed *I Dream of Jeannie*, people surrounded him who would protect him from any missteps. In other words, he had no real grasp of "guerilla filmmaking".

Even though my practical movie-making experience was limited at that point in time, I did understand quite well how micro-budget movies were made. I had had the script of *Death of a Moroon* broken-down and budgeted by a professional, so I knew for a fact that it could be brought in for the money we were requesting.

Our meeting with Edith and her moneyman took place, as I recall, in the Polo Lounge at the Beverly Hills Hotel. I presented our package to him, and he seemed to be impressed with it. Michael kept quiet for most of that time, until we were ready to depart, when out of nowhere, he said: "We *think* we can make this movie on this budget."

Michael is much bigger than me, but at that moment, I wanted to hit him. I had pretty much convinced the moneyman that we were professionals and knew our business, but now Michael had thrown a shadow of doubt into the mix.

I realize that he was just trying to be totally honest, but the problem was that he didn't know what he was talking about and he should have kept his mouth shut.

Sidebar:

Don't you just hate it when you are talking to a salesman in a store, or a service representative on the phone, and they don't know the answer to the question you've asked, so to not appear stupid, they just make up an answer?

When that happens to me, I just say to that person: "It's okay not to know the answer, but please let me speak to somebody who does know."

End of Sidebar.

According to Edith, Michael's comment had not hurt the deal, but everything was being put on hold until after the approaching Thanksgiving Day holiday when we would get a definite answer.

In the meantime, Michael and I were still not comfortable being forced to cast Sophie in the film, and since she was still not happy about doing the nude scene, we decided to put our "plan" into motion.

We insisted that, before we would finalize her casting, Sophie would have to audition in the nude.

True, our hope was that she would refuse to do it, and that would be that. However, there was also a practical reason for our request and Edith, being a professional, understood our reasoning.

We didn't want to be put into a position where we'd cast Sophie, then half way through the filming, she would renege on doing the nude scene. If that happened, she would really have us over a barrel, since our budget would not allow for our re-shooting her scenes with another actress. "If she can audition for us in the nude," we told Edith, "then we're okay that, when it comes to actually shooting the scene, she won't present a problem."

Our plan did not work.

In the Ansaras' pool house, in front of Michael, Edith and me, Sophie plucked up the courage and did the nude audition.

We gave her the part, but that was all for naught, because the money people did not come through with the cash and the project, ultimately, died.

Investors who are *not* in the movie business love the idea of being *in* the film business, taking meetings with all the "glamorous" people that they have watched on the screen. Unfortunately, there are much safer places to invest in than the motion picture industry, which these investors come to realize once it's actually time to put up their money.

There's an amusing coda to this sad story. Three or four years later, I happened to come across a book filled with photographs of ordinary New Yorkers who were posing nude, and one of those pictures was of Sophie.

I was taken totally off-guard when, in 1974, Michael told me that he and Barbara were divorcing. I'm not going to speculate on the reasons for the split of their lengthy marriage, though I'm sure the fact that Barbara had recently lost the child that she was carrying didn't help matters.

Michael didn't want the divorce, and he was in a major state of depression. More than once, I would arrive at my office in the morning to find him waiting for me in the lobby. He just wanted somebody with whom he could talk, and I was happy to be there for him. A few years later, when I split with Terry, he was there for me.

Eventually, however, all things pass. Michael met Beverly Kushida, a delightful, beautiful actress, and they married in 1977. I was an usher at their wedding.

Beverly is absolutely devoted to Michael.

About the same time that they married, Michael's career seemed to slow down a bit, and he made me his personal manager.

I'm not sure if it was me that initially suggested it, or if it was a casting director, but one of us brought forth the idea that Michael should start working without his hairpiece, which was not really a good one. He balked at the proposal at first, but then somebody quoted the Bible to him ("*Pride precedes the fall.*"), and he agreed to dump the rug whenever requested. We had some new headshots taken without the hairpiece and, almost immediately, Michael found himself cast as the lead heavy on an episode of *Kojak* with the equally bald Telly Savalas. More hairless assignments were forthcoming.

In recent years, Michael has even gone all the way, adopting the Yul Brynner look.

Another job that I fielded for Michael was to play Dracula (with hair) in a stage production that would open and play two weeks in San Francisco, then, if successful, go on tour.

The Bram Stoker vampire had long been in the public domain. He had recently had a resurgence in popularity, primarily due to a new Broadway production of the old Bela Lugosi stage play starring Frank Langella, who would later repeat the role in a film version with Laurence Olivier.

The Dracula play in which Michael was being asked to star had no connection whatsoever to the hit show that was then playing in New York. Although adapted from the original Stoker novel, this was a totally different script than the one Langella was doing. Indeed, in this tongue-in-cheek version, Van Helsing, who would be played by Werner Klemperer (*Hogan's Heroes*), was a priest, rather than a professor. Also in the cast was John Fiedler (*12 Angry Men*), who would subsequently become my publicity client.

Since his real name is lost somewhere in the depths of my memory, I will call the producer of this production "Gregory". His plan was to book this *Dracula* into major cities ahead of the Broadway production's national tour, thereby cashing in on audiences who thought they were buying tickets to see the original.

I know that sounds deceitful, but I don't think that he was doing anything illegal. After all, as I said, *Dracula* was in the public domain.

Gregory made us an offer that we couldn't refuse. Michael would get star billing and eight thousand dollars per week, an excellent salary since the top-of-the show fee for guest stars on episodic television then was only twenty-five hundred.

Rehearsals began, under the direction of Ezra Stone, best known for being the original "Henry Aldrich," at the Masonic Temple on Hollywood Boulevard. Everything seemed to be going well until I had a phone conversation with Gregory [*I honestly don't remember exactly what it was about.*] that motivated me to call the local Actor's Equity office and ask them a question.

Steve Kanaly once said of me that I have "a great nose for smelling out a rat," and perhaps this was one of those times.

But, as I said, I don't really remember *what* was bothering me.

A couple hours later, I was having lunch with Michael at the Hamburger Hamlet, located a few doors down the street from the Masonic Temple. Gregory walked into the restaurant, saw me and, suddenly, in the middle of the room, surrounded by waiters and customers, started screaming at me at the top of his lungs. "You son of a bitch," he shouted. "What are you trying to do? Destroy this production?"

Michael and I were totally taken aback by his outburst. Frankly, I thought he was about to physically attack me, and I really had no idea what the hell he was talking about.

Once he calmed down, Gregory told us that he'd received a phone call from Actor's Equity, and they were making demands on him that he didn't like. I don't remember the specifics, but apparently, after I had spoken to him, the union rep's curiosity had been aroused, and he went back and checked the contracts for the production. What he discovered was that the deals Gregory had negotiated with the actors in the show conflicted with one another in various matters, such as billing, and the union was insisting that he correct these issues.

Dracula opened in San Francisco, did not receive the best of critical reviews, and closed two weeks later. In fact, all of the actors' paychecks for the second week of the run bounced and had to be made good with the bond Gregory had posted with Actor's Equity.

And, Gregory?

Michael told me that he did not see him around for the last few days of the run, and neither of us has heard from him since.

Michael continued to work off-and-on, including a key role (and high weekly salary) in the popular 1978 *Centennial* television mini-series, which had been adapted from James Michener's novel. When I began spending more time at my writing than in doing publicity, we agreed that I would stop representing him, but we remained close friends and neighbors, since my Calabasas condo was just three blocks away from his home.

In June of 2001, I was home when I received a call from a *National Enquirer* reporter. She wanted me to talk about Matthew Ansara, Michael and Barbara Eden's then thirty-five year old son. I knew that Matthew had had drug problems in the past, but he had gone through rehab and, as far as I knew, he had cleaned up his act. He was, in fact, supposed to get married (for a second time) in September.

I wasn't about to give this reporter anything she could build upon, so I said something, like "Matthew's doing fine. He and his father are close."

There was a pause—then the woman said, "You haven't heard, have you?"

"Heard what?"

"Matthew Ansara was found dead. It appears to be a drug overdose."

I don't know if I said "goodbye" to that reporter or not. I just slammed down the phone, ran out of my condo, got into my car and sped over to Michael's house. He and Beverly were just pulling into the garage when I arrived. They had been at the funeral home.

What do you say to your friend in a situation like this?

I sat with Michael and Beverly for about a half hour, but then, with Michael being so distraught, I felt it better to leave.

With celebrity parents like Barbara and Michael, there was no question that the press was going to descend on the funeral service like hungry vultures, so even though I was no longer Michael's official publicist or manager, I volunteered to represent him in dealing with the newsmen. I coordinated my efforts with Barbara's manager, Gene Schwam, who I'd worked for on a consulting basis in the past.

I don't think I've ever attended a funeral that has made me feel as sad, nor as angry, as Matthew Ansara's.

Sad, because he was so young.

Angry, because his death was unnecessary, and his stupidity brought so much grief to two parents who loved him.

My friend, Michael Ansara, passed away on July 31, 2013. I will miss him.

14

Flubs & Practical Jokes

I LOVE STORIES ABOUT STAGE MISHAPS.

I'm not talking about the tragic kind of mishap where a light falls and hits an actor on the head. What I'm referring to is when an actor forgets a line or something else goes wrong during a performance, and that actor and the rest of the actors on stage with him have to adjust without breaking character.

Perhaps the funniest flub story I've ever heard, one that I've repeated for years, was told by character actor Fred Clark. If you don't recall the name, you will certainly recognize the familiar face of this tall, bald performer, who often played comic heavies or stodgy bureaucrats in countless television shows and movies, including *Sunset Boulevard*, *Auntie Mame* and *Bells Are Ringing*.

As Clark recounted, he was doing the lead role in a stage play, *Blind Alley*, and he suddenly went blank. He totally forgot his lines. The prompter with script in hand was in the wings on the other side of the stage, so Clark started to ad-lib; working his way over to where the prompter was seated.

Desperate to get a cue that would get him back on track, Clark reached the other side of the stage, cocked his ear toward the wings, only to hear the prompter say, "Sorry, but that's not the right line."

Duh…!

Undoubtedly, the most outrageous stage flub I ever witnessed was in a performance of *The Desperate Hours*, presented at an Equity Waiver theater in West Hollywood. This was a play with which I was familiar. Not only had I seen the national company perform it when I was a kid in Seattle, but I am a fan of the 1955 movie that had starred Humphrey Bogart, Fredric March and Arthur Kennedy.

I was at this new production because one of my publicity clients, Larry Pennell, was playing the Arthur Kennedy role.

Based on a true story, *The Desperate Hours* by Joseph Hayes is about a trio of escaped convicts, led by Bogart in the movie, who take over a suburban household and hold the family hostage, as they plan their final getaway. In the William Wyler-directed film, March played the father and Kennedy was the chief cop trying to catch the criminals.

In the play's climactic moments, one of the convicts has been killed, the police have surrounded the family's home, the wife and grown daughter have been brought to safety, and the father (March) has just forced one of the remaining convicts, played in the movie by Robert Middleton, out of the house into a hail of police bullets.

As the Middleton character is ejected from the house, he drops his gun inside. The father retrieves the weapon, and then goes upstairs to confront the Bogart character, who is still holding March's young son with a gun that he doesn't know is not loaded.

I don't recall the names of the actors who played the convicts in the Equity Waiver production I saw, but the father was Don Dubbins, a skilled performer and a familiar face on episodic television, but perhaps best remembered for a couple of films he made back in the 1950s, *Tribute to a Bad Man* starring Jimmy Cagney and *The D.I.* with Jack Webb.

Now, picture this:

In the performance of the play that I attended, Dubbins forces the convict (the Middleton character) out of the house, but the actor playing that role *neglected to drop his gun*. Dubbins, after desperately looking about the stage for the absent prop, now must mount the stairs and confront the Bogart character *without a weapon*.

Knowing the play as well as I did and realizing what had happened, I cannot express how badly I felt for Dubbins at that moment. In what should have been the play's most intense scene, he was now forced to ask the Bogart character "nicely" to release his son and get out of his house.

I encountered Dubbins at a party a year or two later, and reminded him of that incident, which he said was the "most painful" moment he'd ever spent on stage.

You may recall a weekly 1980s television show, hosted by Dick Clark and Ed McMahon, *TV Bloopers and Practical Jokes*. Most of the one-hour program was devoted to running funny outtakes from movies and television series, but every week the producers would stage one or two, often elaborate, practical jokes with a popular celebrity being the victim.

In one particular month, I not only set two of my favorite clients up as prey for this show, but I also conceived the basis for the shenanigans.

My first target was Steve Kanaly, who was then starring in the *Dallas* television series. The gag was that Steve was being honored as the annual "Cowboy of the Year" by a local group comprised of Western movie buffs, but neither the award nor the group actually existed. They were all a figment of my and the show's producers' imaginations.

The award banquet was being held at a first-rate hotel in Universal City. There were perhaps fifty or more guests in attendance, as well as Steve's co-star on *Dallas* and my former client, Howard Keel, who would be making the presentation, since he had won the "award" the previous year.

Remember, everybody in the room was in on the gag except Steve. The "guests" were all actors or extras. Even Steve's wife, Brent, had been a conspirator in the plot. I had phoned their house for the past few weeks when Steve was at the studio, in order to work out the details of the prank.

Everything unfolded perfectly at the hotel banquet room. Steve, Brent, Howard and I were on the dais. In fact, I was wearing a hidden microphone in order to catch Steve's reaction to what was about to happen.

Steve did appear a bit amused when he heard one the speakers discuss the group's political agenda. They wanted Congress to pass a "Horses on the Highway" law, which would provide a separate lane on all freeways for horses.

Next, Howard presented Steve with the actual trophy, and his jaw dropped. It was a white, life-sized statue of a horse. You could tell by the look on Steve's face what he was thinking: "Where the hell am I going to put that?"

But, the real zinger was saved for last.

The president of this fictional group came to the podium and thanked Steve profusely for "his generous contribution" to their "Horses on the Highway" fund.

Steve's expression read, "What contribution?"

The president then produced a blown up copy of a check for $25,000.00…signed by Steve's business manager.[1]

Steve didn't say anything, but his face seemed to turn green.

---

1. It was a real check that I had obtained for the gag, but payment on it had already been stopped.

When he was seated back at the head table, and so that my hidden microphone could pick up his reaction, I said, "That was really generous of you, Steve."

"We'll talk about it later," he grumbled.

Moments later, Howard got up and announced, "Steve, you've been a victim of *TV Bloopers and Practical Jokes.*"

Steve grinned. It was like he had just won (or saved) $25,000.00.

Two or three weeks later, I trapped Abe Vigoda in an even more elaborate gag.

Abe had played a major role in *The Godfather*, as well as several other Mafia parts during his career. Once a cop, saying his face "looked familiar," even stopped him and was about to check him out until Abe explained he was an actor.

That was the basis for this joke: Abe Vigoda being mistaken as being a hoodlum.

I told Abe that he and his wife, Bea, were to be my guests at a new upscale restaurant that I was representing. Abe was somewhat reluctant to go, but since Bea was in on the joke, she saw to it that he had no choice.

Wives rule, right?

Once again, this was a phony restaurant, set up by the show's producers. All of the customers and waiters were actors, and the only person *not* in on the prank was Abe.

We hadn't been seated in the restaurant for five minutes when a bunch of uniformed police officers, all actors, walked in and announced, "This is a raid!"

Everybody was asked to go into the back room where it was discovered that illegal gambling…roulette, craps, Blackjack…was in progress.

At first, Abe was amused. He had just come into the restaurant to have dinner. What was going on in the back room had nothing to do with him, he thought.

Then, suddenly, as the police led them out in handcuffs, the dealers and other people who were working the gambling operation started pointing their fingers directly at Abe, saying things like, "We're down about five grand tonight, Abe," or "You said this was for charity," or "Abe, you promised to get me a lawyer."

Abe didn't know what to say, particularly when the police started to surround him and ask, "Do you own this operation, sir?"

"I'm an actor," he tried to explain. "Don't you know me from my shows, *Barney Miller* and *Fish*?"

But, the "cops" weren't buying it. The grilling continued, and Abe kept trying to talk his way out of this testy situation.

Me? I was cracking up listening to the exchange. I had to turn away, so that Abe wouldn't see me laughing.

Finally, a mock television crew arrived on the scene and asked Abe, who at that point probably felt he was headed for jail, for a comment. He, again, tried to explain that he was on television, but then the "reporter" let him off the hook. "Have you ever been on *TV Bloopers and Practical Jokes*?" she asked.

"No, I've never been on that show," Abe replied.

"Well, you are now."

Abe started to laugh, and said: "This is the best acting I have ever seen."

From time to time, I'm not above pulling somebody's leg on my own. My 2008 book, *Once Upon a Time in Hollywood: From the Secret Files of Harry Pennypacker* was most certainly a spoof of Hollywood's Golden Age and the tabloid press that covered it.

Yet, despite the fact that the stories in it are so outrageous and bizarre (e.g. the Land of Oz was a real place, or W.C. Fields and Mae West were the same person), there are people who have, indeed, asked me if these accounts were true.

Now, when I sign a copy of the book, I always write: *"Don't believe everything you read."*

Then, there are the occasions when I've been I've been in a mischievous mood with a group of people discussing actors or theatre, and I'll say something like, "Don't you think that Edwin Booth was a terrific actor?"

You would be surprised at how many people have agreed with me.

15

Difficult & Unusual Clients

NOT EVERY CLIENT A PUBLICIST takes on is as pleasant to work with as almost all of the personalities I've been talking about. Some of them are as difficult to get along with as Michael Conrad was…or even worse.

Others were not "difficult." They were just "different."

Peter Hurkos, for example, was a world-renowned psychic, who even worked with the police on the infamous "Boston Strangler" case.

I met him strictly by accident. Back in the early 1970s when I was collecting movies on 16mm, I took my projector in for repair and, as I was leaving, a stranger who was entering the shop stopped me and said, "You're a film collector."

Since these were the days before home video when owning 16mm movies was not quite kosher, I was initially hesitant to respond. After all, he could have been a representative of the major studios, looking to snag a film pirate.

"I'm Peter Hurkos," the man said, introducing himself.

"*The* Peter Hurkos?" I said, much impressed.

"Yes," he replied. "*The* Peter Hurkos."

Peter and I hit it off right away. We shared a love of movies, though our tastes differed. Whereas I liked films with Bogart, Cagney and Edward G. Robinson, Peter was a major fan of Mario Lanza, who was not a particular favorite of mine.

I visited his home often and, virtually every time I was there, a Hollywood celebrity or two, like actress Joanne Dru or actor Albert Salmi, who had played Peter on a television show, was also present.

(Like Christian Brando and Gig Young, Albert Salmi is another brief acquaintance who would later commit murder. In 1990, he would kill his wife and then himself in their Spokane, Washington, home.)

At one point in our relationship, Hurkos' wife, Stephany, who pretty much managed his career, asked if I would be interested in handling Peter's publicity. I was, of course, interested, and part of my fee was going to be a free psychic reading from Peter.

A word about psychics:

Personally, I think that 95% of the people who claim to be "psychic" are phonies, particularly the ones who advertise or work out of storefronts. They're like the character on TV's *The Mentalist*. They are experts at reading people, and they know exactly what to say in order to make their "mark" believe that they have a special power.

On the other hand, there seem to be a few gifted people, like Peter, who by touching something or via some other method, can get an uncanny insight into a person's past…or even their future. In their mind's eye, they will see a "picture" of an event, a person or whatever. What they tell you is not necessarily accurate as to what happened or will happen, but *their interpretation* of what they've seen.

As Peter described it to me: "When you are riding on a train, you only see the scenery as it passes by your window. However, with me, it's like I'm sitting on top of the train, and I can see the scenery that we've already passed and also what is up ahead."

My late client, comedian Jackie Vernon, once told me about a party he attended in New York where a palm reader was present. The woman was there to give free readings, but when one particular guest presented his palm, she looked at it, and then pushed it away. "I don't want to read you," she said.

Two days later, that guest was walking down the street when an out-of-control car jumped the curb and killed him.

Makes you wonder, doesn't it?

Peter did my reading, and told me things that he could not have known. In fact, many of the items that I gave him to touch were photographs in a manila envelope, so he had no way of knowing what the images were.

Unfortunately, our publicity/client relationship did not go as well as the reading. It lasted about a month. Sometimes it's just much easier to be friends with somebody than to be in a business relationship.

During my time as a publicist, I was approached on more than one occasion to represent producers of pornographic films. I had always turned down those accounts; not because I'm a "prude," which I'm definitely not, but because I felt that representing an XXX-rated producer would detract from any positive image I might have in the Hollywood community.

However, during my divorce proceedings with Terry, I suddenly lost two or three high paying clients within the period of a month, so when this guy who made porn movies came to me, I decided to consider his request for representation.

What surprised me was how easy it was to get major press for this guy. Indeed, important columnists like James Bacon and Vernon Scott were delighted to have lunch with him…particularly when he brought along one or two of the girls who appeared in his pictures.

"I'm an 'actress'," one of the girls said during an interview. "I'll perform with two guys, other women, but I will not do it with an animal."

Let's just leave it at that.

Barbara Nichols was a good actress who, because of her looks, was usually cast as a blowsy blonde in films like *Sweet Smell of Success* and *The Pajama Game*.

She was a client for a month or two in the early 1970s, but we did not get along. She had a drinking problem, and every time she'd had one too many, she'd get angry, and start screaming at me over the phone.

Having had to deal with a few women in my life that liked the bottle too much, I let her go.

Sometimes however, since you've been hired to handle a client's public image, you just have to deal with their over indulgence the best you can.

I'd booked an actor client on a television talk show. What I didn't know was that the coffee mug he was drinking from on-camera was filled with vodka. During the commercial breaks, he would send the assistant director out to the green room to refill the mug. I had to drive him home that night in his own car.

I remember that incident because it was the only time in my life that I've driven a Rolls Royce.

Nell Carter was another client that I only represented for a month or two, several years before she starred in the hit sitcom, *Gimme a Break!*

She had recently won the Tony Award for *Ain't Misbehavin'*, and was about to star in the Los Angeles production of that musical. Charles Nelson Reilly's business manager also represented her, and he had recommended me.

Nell and I got along okay. There were no real issues between us. She was nice to me, but I always sensed that there was something "wrong" about her. And there was. As I learned later, she had a drug problem.

When I phoned her business manager to inquire as to when I would be getting a check for my second month of publicity services, he informed me that there was not enough money in Nell's account to pay me yet. Apparently, rather than letting her weekly salary go directly to the business manager so that he could take care of her obligations, Nell had been picking up the check at the box-office before it could be mailed.

I can only imagine how that money was spent.

Then, there were the clients that I had to sue in small claims court.

I'm proud to say that I never lost a case in small claims court, though I was only able to collect about half the judgments that I was awarded.

In or out of the entertainment world, there are people who make a career of not paying their obligations, and we all know some of these people.

For me, taking a client to small claims was not really about the money, which was never enough to make or break me. It was always about the principle.

In most instances, when you have a dispute with a client, you can sit down and work it out, as I did with Michael Conrad. I may not have liked the solution in that particular instance, but we were able to reach a compromise.

The people who I sued basically told me to "shove it," which is not a wise thing to do with me.

One of these deadbeats was a well known and, at this writing, still active, rather controversial, comedian, so I will just call him "Funnyman".

Funnyman owed me about $1200.00 for my services, which he refused to pay. He did not even appear in court, but sent his representative, who was promptly ruled against by the judge.

Collecting this award, however, was another matter. Funnyman lived in New York and, without spending a few hundred dollars; I had no way tracing his assets. So, I let the matter rest for a year or two, and then I read in the paper that Funnyman was going to play a weekend club date in Los Angeles.

Ah ha! This was the perfect opportunity to collect my money. I would have the sheriff's office go to the club and grab his salary.

I got a writ of execution from the court, and then took it to the local sheriff's office. The deputy behind the counter looked at the paper and laughed. "Wow," he said, "we've already got over a dozen of these to serve on this guy."

None of the people who had sued Funnyman collected a dime off of that club date. He was too smart for that. He'd arranged for his fee to be paid in advance to him in New York.

I'm sure he was proud of himself.

One afternoon, I got a phone call from a personal manager who wanted me to represent a client, who was a "writer".

This guy was as much a writer as I am a brain surgeon. Actually, he claimed to be a former Mob hitman who had been hired by some producer to serve as technical advisor for a Mafia movie he was making. The manager, who (I believe) was also helping to pay this guy's living expenses, felt that there could be more work of this sort for his client, and he figured that with publicity that work would materialize.

I met with both manager and client, but I was hesitant to take on the account. "Hitman" seemed like a nice enough guy, but unless more work was forthcoming, I didn't see how I would ever get paid. "Don't worry about it," the manager said. "I will guarantee your fee." Apparently, a large check from the movie that Hitman had worked on previously was forthcoming.

A few weeks passed in which I was able to get my new client some stories in the press, but then Hitman had some sort of falling out with his manager, and the manager informed me that he was rescinding his guarantee. Since Hitman didn't have any money of his own, my only recourse was against the manager, who I ultimately sued. After all, I would never have taken on the account had it not been for that guarantee.

Hitman actually appeared in court as my witness, and once the manager admitted that he did, in fact, guarantee payment, the judge ruled in my favor, though he cut the amount of the award to about half of what I was asking.

The manager appealed the ruling, but when he did not show up in court for that second hearing, the new judge overruled the first one and gave me everything that I'd originally requested which, as I recall, was about $1500.00.

Still the manager would not pay me, so since a small claims ruling is good for ten years, my lawyer suggested that we put a judgment lien on all real estate in Los Angeles County, as well as neighboring Orange, San Bernardino and Ventura Counties, which was owned by anybody with the same name as the manager. The attorney assured me that if property owned by another person with the same name as the manger was affected, that particular lien could be easily and quickly removed.

Three or four years passed, then one day my attorney received a call from an escrow company that was handling the sale of a piece of property owned by the manager. They wanted to know what the lien was all about. My lawyer told them, and that was the last he heard about it.

I can only assume that either the sale fell through or, since this manager was a vindictive person, he blew the sale altogether…just so that he would not have to pay me.

I wouldn't put it past him.

Perhaps the most interesting case that I brought to small claims court involved a young actress and her mother, who happened to be the daughter of a famous Broadway scenic designer. The young girl, who I'll call "Sally," had recently co-starred in a popular teen "coming of age" comedy, and she had some heat going for her.

I agreed to represent Sally on a percentage deal, but before she signed the contract, I asked her mother, who I'll call "Gertrude," if her daughter was eighteen. After all, if she were under age, the agreement would not be valid. Gertrude assured me that Sally was eighteen, and the contract was signed.

Over the next few weeks, I arranged for Sally to be interviewed and photographed for several popular teen fan magazines (e.g. *Tiger Beat*), and at one of these lunch meetings she brought along a girl friend.

While we were sitting in the restaurant, waiting for the reporter to arrive, I listened to these two girls talk (and giggle) to each other, and it suddenly struck me that I'd been had. There was no way that Sally was eighteen years old. These were a pair of young teenagers. Indeed, when I was married to Terry, I had two teenage stepdaughters, so I knew what teenage girls sounded like.

I don't recall how I confirmed this, but I did find out later that day that Sally was only sixteen.

"I don't want to make an issue out of this," I told Gertrude when I called her, "but, I need you to come into my office and co-sign Sally's contract. That will make everything legal."

Gertrude agreed to come in, but when after two or three more phone calls she still hadn't appeared, I decided to sue her and Sally for the money I would have charged had they hired me for a flat monthly fee, rather than on a percentage.

The judge gave me a judgment against Gertrude, but not Sally. I believe that was proper, since Gertrude was the "adult" in this matter and had initiated the lie.

A week or two after the trial, Gertrude paid me the money.

"Revenge is a meal best served cold."

Nobody seems to be totally sure who originated that delicious phrase, which is often attributed to the Mafia. However, in concluding this chapter, I must tell you about an incident that occurred while I was in the check cashing business for over two years.

For those of you who didn't read the first memoir or, if you did, don't recall that detour in my life, I'm talking about the early 1990s when I was "transitioning" from the public relations business to becoming a full time writer.

During the first week that I had the business and was still learning the ropes, I cashed a check for fifty dollars, but after the customer was gone, I realized that I'd screwed up. The check was, in fact, for only fifty *cents*, but it was written in such a way that you had to look closely to see the exact amount.

I had a copy of the customer's I.D., so I phoned him on several occasions and asked him to return and do the right thing, but he never did.

Lesson learned. Instead of depositing the check into my bank account, I filed it away and forgot about it.

Two years passed, and one night…just about the time that I was planning to close…a customer came to the window of my kiosk with his payroll check for several hundred dollars. His name rang a bell in my memory. I went to the filing cabinet and, sure enough, it was the same guy who had stuck me with the check for fifty cents.

Yes!

I played it cool. I had him endorse the payroll check and give me his driver's license to photocopy. Then, I showed him the original check and said, "You owe me fifty dollars."

"What!?!"

"You came back to the wrong place," I said with a grin.

He knew exactly what I was talking about. He tried to object, but I told him that I was keeping his check and also his driver's license until he paid me the fifty dollars. He didn't have the cash on him, so he called a friend who was there in about a half hour with the money.

Cash in hand, I gave him back both the license and the payroll check, and told him to go elsewhere. I didn't want his business.

As I said: *"Revenge is a meal best served cold."*

16

Musings About Actors

"I couldn't be a director.
I couldn't put up with actors for twenty minutes.
I'd go right out of my mind."
— Spencer Tracy

I LIKE ACTORS. Some of my dearest friends are actors. But, Spencer Tracy was right. Actors *are* a different breed of cat.

I should talk !?!

Writers aren't the most "normal" people either; then again I'll get to that matter in the next chapter.

I've worked with actors in virtually every professional capacity possible: publicist, writer, director, producer and, of course, as a fellow actor. No matter how many years they've been in the profession or how big a star they might be, all actors have one thing in common: insecurity.

Again, *I should talk!?!*

The late David Niven (*The Guns of Navarone, Separate Tables*), an Oscar winner, once said that, throughout his entire, hugely successful career, he always feared that his current job would be his last.

That's not as paranoid as it sounds. The truth is that any job can be an actor's last. It is a tenuous profession.

The other day, I was chatting with my friend, actress Marian Hailey, who quit acting thirty years ago to become a licensed psychotherapist, and I quipped that she'd gone from working with one kind of crazy person to working with another.

Remember *Shakespeare in Love*?

Even though that Academy Award-winning movie is set centuries in the past, it contains many truths about actors and the theatrical profession.

You'll recall that the plot of the film revolves around the first production of Shakespeare's *Romeo and Juliet*. In one of my favorite moments, the character who plays the "Nurse" in the play within a play is asked what *Romeo and Juliet* is about, and he answers: "It's about this nurse...."

Is it any secret that actors usually seem to view a play or screenplay from the standpoint of their own role, large or small?

When I first began my public relations business and was running my "A Press Agent for $25.00" ads, a lot of actors came through my door that had played supporting and even bit parts in films and on television. The veterans like Reed Hadley, James Griffith, Don Keefer and others were pragmatic about their work and their place in the entertainment industry, but many of the younger performers would greatly enhance their activities.

"I played Rod Steiger's deputy in *In the Heat of the Night*, and I was a pioneer with Kirk Douglas and Robert Mitchum in *The Way West*," a young actor told me when we first met.

Sounds impressive, right?

Rod Steiger had several deputies in that Academy Award-winning picture, including this actor who had about three lines, and in *The Way West*, he was not much more than a silent extra. Indeed, if I hadn't known him, I would never even have noticed him in that Western.

Then, there was the actress who took a half page ad in *Daily Variety* to promote her appearance that night on a television show. Unlike Aram Katcher whose "Napoleon Bonaparte" character was, at least, central to the *I Dream of Jeannie* episode in which he'd appeared, her role was, literally, a one-line bit. She played a receptionist who, when one of the series' regulars came to her desk, picked up the phone and said something like, "Mr. Jones is here."

Trade ads are expensive. As a publicist, I often designed ads (with the help of an artist) for my clients when they had something really worthwhile to promote. *But, a one line bit!?!*

Realistically, most of the time in the film business, a job is *just* a job. You say the words. You take the money. You go home.

Even when you do have a project worth talking about, what looks good on paper does not always translate well to the screen.

One of my favorite clients was Henry Darrow (*High Chaparral*), a marvelous raconteur. He was signed by Disney to star in a new television series, *Zorro and Son*, a spoof of their classic 1950s series with Guy Williams. I thought it was a hilarious concept with great potential.

Planning our publicity campaign, I would talk to Henry on the phone quite often, and he would tell me about the script for the following week's episode. He'd describe it in such detail that he would have me laughing out loud. I knew that this was going to be the funniest show on television.

Boy, was I wrong!

I attended the gala press party at the studio where the pilot episode was screened.

It was a disaster. Whoever directed that episode, as well as the succeeding four episodes that were filmed, knew absolutely nothing about directing comedy. The actors were fine, but the scenes that Henry had hilariously described to me were so ineptly shot and edited that they just lay there like a blob of soggy mud.

The show got terrible reviews and disappeared from the network schedule after the fifth episode aired.

Remember what veteran character actor Edmund Gwenn (*Miracle on 34th Street*) said on his deathbed?

"Dying is easy. Playing comedy is hard."

Since we're discussing actors and their insecurities, I'm reminded of an actress who I directed in one of my one-person stage plays. She's a nice person, so I will not embarrass her by mentioning her name, nor the title of the play. I'll call her "Gloria."

Gloria was perfect casting for this role, and she was actually a good actress, but perhaps the most insecure actress with whom I've ever worked. She did not trust me as the writer-director, and worse still; she did not seem to trust her own abilities. If somebody would give her a suggestion as to how to read a line or play a scene, she would take it.

The afternoon of opening night, we had a final dress rehearsal of the play, and she was perfect. I couldn't have been happier when I left to go home, have dinner and change for the evening's festivities.

What I didn't know until later is that, after I'd left, she ran through the play again for a director friend of hers, and he suggested a number of changes, which she employed for that night's performance. On other occasions, different friends would make further suggestions that she would follow and, at one performance, she got so mixed up that she went totally blank on stage; not a good thing to happen, particularly in a one-person play…with no off-stage prompter.

"Do you have any questions?" she asked the audience after a long, uncomfortable moment of silence. Luckily, I was sitting in the last row, and I called out a question that got her back on track. The performance continued without further incident.

The moral of this story is that, right or wrong, a ship can only have one master, and a play can only have one director.

Do you want to know how to make an actor, even a big star, your momentary "best friend"?

Just mention one of their "forgotten children".

Every artist, whether they are an actor, a writer, composer or whatever has one or more "forgotten children". They are those special works (e.g. a movie, a screenplay, a song) that came from the heart and flopped. Critics hated them and/or the public ignored them.

My late client, lyricist Paul Francis Webster, always claimed that "Love Is a Many Splendored Thing," which he wrote with Sammy Fain, was his all time favorite song. Yes, the song won the Academy Award and is now a well-known standard, but before that it was Webster's "orphan". Virtually every major recording artist hated it, including Nat "King" Cole, Eddie Fisher, Perry Como, Tony Martin and even Webster's neighbor, Doris Day.

Nobody would touch the song until, in order to get a commercial single, 20th Century-Fox, who had commissioned Webster and Fain to write the number for their forthcoming movie of the same name, subsidized an entire album for a new group, The Four Aces, after which the song took off.

I attended the premiere of *MacArthur* (1977) with my client Dan O'Herlihy, who played "FDR" opposite Gregory Peck's "General Douglas MacArthur" in the picture. At the dinner party that followed, I was standing next to Dan with a group of people that included Jack Lemmon.

Although I'd been at events where he'd been present before, Lemmon and I had never been formally introduced. When we were that night, I mentioned how much I'd enjoyed *Alex and the Gypsy*, a film of his that had been released about a year earlier that had bombed. He beamed a warm smile, turned to me and gave me his full attention; told me how special that picture was to him and how disappointed he was that the public had ignored it. We talked for several minutes, until they started serving dinner.

A similar incident occurred when I visited Dan on the set of *The Last Starfighter*. I was there as his publicist, but my real reason for coming that day was to meet his co-star, Robert Preston. I'd been a fan of his ever since I'd seen the movie version of *The Music Man* and, as mentioned in an earlier chapter, I was lucky enough to see him and Mary Martin on stage in *I Do! I Do!*

Preston was an affable man who, like with Jack Lemmon, gave me his undivided attention when I mentioned one of his "forgotten children". He even did a virtual double take.

The show that I cited was *We Take the Town*, a Broadway-bound musical about Pancho Villa (played by Preston) that had "closed out of town" in 1962.[1]

Preston told me how fond he was of that show, and that he was so surprised that anybody remembered it. We chatted until he was called to do his scene.

Incidentally, before we totally leave the subject of Jack Lemmon, he used to tell a story: a perfect illustration of the difference between stage and film acting.

The actor was making his first picture, *It Should Happen to You*, directed by George Cukor. On his first day of filming, Cukor kept yelling "Cut," then coming up to Lemmon and giving him a one word direction, "Less!"

This went on for many, many takes until a frustrated Lemmon turned to Cukor and said, "Don't you want me to act at all?"

"That right," the director replied.

When I met with Janet Leigh in her home to do a pre-interview for the on-camera chat I would be doing with her a few days later for the American Movie Classics cable channel, we spent several hours talking about many things, but she was most appreciative when I told her that I thought she was treated badly by the producers of her 1963 movie, *Bye Bye Birdie*.

That film adaptation of the Tony-winning Broadway musical was totally restructured; its focus changed from the original stage production in order to spotlight Ann-Margret and to appeal to a teen audience. Janet Leigh was no stranger to musical comedy (*Walking My Baby Back Home*,

---

1. In doing research for this book, I discovered that two of my other publicity clients, Mark Lenard, who co-starred in the *Planet of the Apes* television series, and actor-singer-Broadway star Art Lund (*The Most Happy Fella*) were also in the cast of that show. Lund was Preston's standby.

My Sister Eileen), yet her role, which was played on stage by Chita Rivera and is, in fact, the lead, was cut down to its bare bones, with almost all of her character's musical numbers eliminated.

Ann-Margret may have been terrific and the movie did make a ton of money, but the picture itself was mediocre and, at times, so juvenile in its humor that it was difficult to watch; a pale shadow of what it could have been had it conformed more closely to its stage origins.

"Michael," Janet said, as I left that day, "you made me very happy with your remarks."

There are times when it is perhaps not wise to mention a favorite film or play to an actor.

I once did a telephone interview with Cary Grant about the *Topper* movies, which were going to be the subject of a chapter in *One Good Film Deserves Another*, my book about movie sequels. He had starred in the first film of the trilogy, and he graciously spent several minutes recounting his memories of the movie to me. "You're going to have to take everything I tell you as fact," he quipped, "because everybody else involved is dead."

After I'd finished my questions, I commented that one of my favorite Cary Grant movies was *Arsenic and Old Lace*. "How can you like that?" he snapped. "That's one of the worst pictures I ever made."

You never know.

When you're in the entertainment business, friends, clients and colleagues are always inviting you to special screenings for their latest film or to a performance of a stage play in which they are either appearing in or directing. Hopefully, the movie or play is either terrific or, at the very least, somewhat entertaining, but there are times when even the most talented person gets involved with a turkey.

So, what do you do when that happens?

The film has ended. The lights in the theater or screening room have come up. Now, you have to walk to the exit.

And, who is standing right there?

Your friend; the person who invited you.

You could sneak out through a side exit, if there is one, and avoid him altogether.

But, if one isn't available, you're stuck. You've got to walk up to the door and face him.

What do you say?

"This was biggest piece of shit I've ever seen in my life?"

Not if you want to maintain a decent relationship with this person.

You could lie, and say that it was "wonderful" and will win every Academy Award, but the truth is that, deep inside, this person already knows that his film or play had problems, so he would know that you were being insincere.

Then, there's the neutral assessment, like "It was amazing," or "I've never seen anything like this in my life," but those are just as bad as the others.

I think that character actor Keenan Wynn had the best solution when faced with this dilemma. He'd walk up to his friend, smile, give him a light, glancing punch on the shoulder, shake his hand and say "Son of a bitch!"

That response is certainly open to interpretation.

I stepped into an elevator one day, and immediately recognized the only other occupant. He was an actor, Casey Adams, who had played secondary, albeit key, roles in many movies of the 1950s. Perhaps he is best remembered as Jean Peters' husband in the classic Marilyn Monroe thriller, *Niagara*.

In the early 1960s, Adams reverted to using his real name, Max Showalter, professionally, and since I had his undivided attention in that elevator, I decided to ask him why he would drop "Casey Adams" since he was so well established in the business under that name.

"I hated that name," he said with a guffaw. "I was under contract to Fox, and they chose it. So, when I went freelance, I went back to my own name because I'm 'Max Showalter,' not 'Casey Adams.'"

"Didn't that hurt your career?" I wanted to know.

"Not at all," he said. "Casey Adams was never a star, and producers and casting people knew what I could do."

As Max Showalter, the former Casey Adams played the stage role of "Horace Vandergelder" in *Hello, Dolly!* more than 3,000 times opposite such ladies as Carol Channing, Betty Grable, Ginger Rogers, and Betsy Palmer, and also did television and films, most notably playing "Grandpa Fred" in *Sixteen Candles* (1984).

Barbara Hershey, who was a publicity client for a few months about the time her breakout movie, *Last Summer* (1969), was released, also changed her professional name for a short while to "Barbara Seagull," but that didn't work for her. Unlike Showalter, Barbara was a star and, aside from her magnificent acting abilities, producers who hired her were also paying for a star's name to advertise on their marquees.

"Barbara Seagull" was a virtual unknown; therefore I can only assume that the reappearance of "Barbara Hershey" was a practical decision on her part.

Some actors just don't know when they are better off. Allen Jenkins (*A Slight Case of Murder, Destry Rides Again*), one of the most popular character actors of the 1930s and 40s, told me that when he wanted out of his long-term contract at Warner Brothers, the studio would not release him. He figured that he would make more money and get better roles if he free-lanced.

One morning, he arrived on the set and pretended to be falling down drunk, continuing that charade for the rest of the day. That worked. When his scenes for that picture were finished, the studio fired him.

Jenkins continued to work in Hollywood, mostly in "B" pictures, but not at Warner Brothers. His roles didn't get any better and, although I can't be sure, it's doubtful that his annual income ever equaled what he had been earning under contract.

The best actor that I ever worked with professionally was, without doubt, the late Sid Conrad, who starred in the original production of my one-person play, *Tracy*. Sid was in his early sixties when I cast him in that role, and, within two minutes of the curtain going up every night, audiences forgot that they were watching an actor and believed that they were in the presence of the real Spencer Tracy. He got rave reviews for that performance, and deservedly so.

Sid and I got along pretty well. During rehearsals he suggested some dialogue cuts that I accepted, and those adjustments did, in fact, result in a better final script. But, like with Richard Castellano and Michael Conrad, I sensed a deep-seated anger in Sid that, though not overt, was directed toward me during the production, most likely because I, as the playwright and uncredited producer of this show, was the resident "suit".[2]

On the other hand, after the play had closed, he was extremely genial whenever we spoke and, on one or two occasions, I attended a barbeque or other social event at his home.

I could definitely understand Sid's frustrations. Here was an extremely gifted veteran actor who had never been able to break into the "big time," but had been relegated to spending his entire professional ca-

---

2. In show business, actors often refer to management, producers, money and business people as "the suits".

reer doing local or regional theatre, commercials and episodic television, such as a two or three line role as an admiral on *JAG* or a congressman on *The West Wing*.

Nevertheless, watching Sid Conrad breathe life into my play every night was an unforgettable experience. It was like the time when I was back in high school and saw Edward Everett Horton doing a play at Seattle's Cirque Playhouse, milking every possible laugh out of the audience. In both instances, I was in the presence of a master actor.

Speaking of master actors, I must mention Nina Foch (*My Name is Julia Ross, An American in Paris, Executive Suite*).

I first met Nina when I interviewed her for my book about Paul Muni, with whom she had worked in *A Song to Remember* (1945). She told me that, being relatively new in the business when she did the film, the Academy Award-winning actor (*The Story of Louis Pasteur*) had taken an interest in her and, one day, had asked her, quite bluntly: "Do you want to be a good actress or a professional whore?"

Recalled Nina: "In his own way, Muni was telling me that I could continue working in films and learn nothing or continue to study my craft and become an accomplished performer. The talk had a profound effect on my life and career."

When Nina became a publicity client, she was acting only occasionally. In fact, while she was with me, she received an Emmy nomination for her performance on an episode of *Lou Grant*. Primarily though, she was a highly respected teacher of other actors, many of whom were enjoying successful careers. In a class session that I visited, for example, I noticed that Jim Backus (*Gilligan's Island*) was in attendance.

Nina passed away in 2008. She had a couple of credos that I will never forget:

1. "Not every script you get is going to be 'Shakespeare'. It may, indeed, be a piece of shit. But, as an actor, you approach that script as if it were 'Shakespeare,' and you will not go wrong."
2. "Fame and fortune are fine, but the most satisfying thing in this business is *The Work*. Concentrate on and enjoy doing The Work and everything else will fall into place."

Wise words.

17

Musings About Writers

"Substitute 'damn' every time you're inclined to write 'very'; your editor will delete it and the writing will be just as it should be."

— Mark Twain

WOULD YOU BELIEVE THAT, just before I started writing this chapter, I did a search of the preceding chapters and eliminated almost every use of the word "very"?

I only wish I'd also done that with some of my previously published books, but that's all water under the bridge.

We writers, even the most prosperous in our profession, do tend to develop some bad habits.

My late former father-in-law, renowned comedy writer Ray Singer, was no exception. He, too, developed writing practices that were difficult to break.

In his day, Singer was one of the top sitcom writers in the business. His credits date back to the Golden Days of radio when he wrote for the *Alice Faye/Phil Harris Show*, and in television, he wrote for the likes of Danny Thomas, Joey Bishop and Lucille Ball. He even co-wrote Rowan and Martin's 1969 movie, *The Maltese Bippy*.

Ray was a gentle man, who was pretty much (involuntarily) retired when I met him. Despite the fact that my marriage to his daughter, Laurie, didn't work out, he was always extremely kind to me. Years before I actually made my first sale as a screenwriter, he tried to help me by introducing me to some of his still active, influential friends, and his cousin, Carol Schild, did become my agent…and she was quite a good one.

Ray's "dream" was to have a stage play produced on Broadway, which was the one medium he had yet to make a part of in his impressive career. Since (Clark) *Gable*, my first one-person play had just been successfully produced locally in an Equity-waiver theater, Ray asked me to read his play to see what I thought of it.

It was, as I recall, a funny play, but it did have a major problem: The characters were not well defined.

Ray was a sitcom writer, and in episodes of those weekly half-hour series, there was no pressing need to flesh-out the characters, because the audience already knew who they were and everything about them. They didn't care about what made Lucy "tick". They just wanted her to be funny.

Unfortunately, Ray used a sitcom approach in writing his stage play. He did not develop these original characters, so there was no way to really know who they were, where they came from, or why an audience should care about them. It was like the play began with the second act.

When I tried to discuss this encumbrance with my father-in-law, he didn't want to listen. After all, I was just an aspiring screenwriter without credits, so what did I know?

Ray died in 1992. His play, as far as I know, is still unproduced.

During one of our frequent talks, Ray gave me some excellent advice on how to handle a troublesome actor.

During the mid-1950s, he and his writing partner, Dick Chevillat, had created and produced a television series, *It's a Great Life*, which starred Michael O'Shea, William Bishop, James Dunn and Frances Bavier. O'Shea, according to Ray, was constantly complaining about one thing or another, and at one point, he even threatened to walk off the show. "So, we wrote him out of one episode," Ray recalled, "and the next week he was back, hat in hand."

Even composers sometimes find that they have to go head-to-head with the artists chosen to present their work. My client, Marty Paich, one of Hollywood's most respected arrangers and music directors, invited me to observe one of his recording sessions where Don Cherry was going to sing a ballad that would play over the end credits of *Will Penny*, a 1968 Paramount Western starring Charlton Heston.

Veteran composer David Raksin (*Laura, The Bad and the Beautiful*) had written the song, and he was not happy with Cherry's phrasing of the lyrics. After the first couple of takes, he walked into the studio and attempted to explain to the singer the proper way to do the song. Cherry did not appear to appreciate the input, and the exchange became a bit heated.

After all, what did Raksin know? He was only the composer.

Like with Ray Singer, when you reach a certain age…which seems to get younger as the years pass…work dries up for even the most accomplished writers. I think that happens because the producers and other people making hiring decisions are getting younger, and they don't feel comfortable hiring their "fathers".

There was a boarding kennel near my home in Calabasas Park where I used to leave my pets when I had to go out of town on business. The man behind the counter there owned the place with his wife. He was Sam Perrin, one of Jack Benny's top writers since the late comedian's days in radio and one of the most revered comedy writers in the entertainment business.

I asked him why he wasn't still writing.

"I guess the young guys don't think I'm funny anymore," he said.

W.R. Burnett was the "father" of the modern American gangster genre. Not only did he write *Little Caesar*, the novel upon which the classic Edward G. Robinson film was adapted, but his name can also be found in the writing credits of pictures like *Scarface* (1932), *High Sierra*, *This Gun for Hire* and *The Asphalt Jungle*, as well as non-crime movies, *Dark Command*, *Wake Island*, for which he was nominated for an Oscar, *Yellow Sky* and *The Great Escape*. He was, indeed, one of the finest writers of his generation.

I became acquainted with Mr. Burnett when I was researching my book, *Make It Again, Sam: A Survey of Movie Remakes*. I was including a chapter in that volume about the three versions of *High Sierra*, so I contacted him for an interview.[1]

During our phone conversations, he mentioned that it had been many years since he'd seen either *Little Caesar* or *Scarface*. I happened to have 16mm prints of both those films, and anxious to meet this legendary writer in person, I invited him to my home in Agoura Hills for a screening; an invitation he readily accepted. Since his eyesight was failing, his son drove him that night.

---

1. Aside from the original picture in 1941 that had starred Humphrey Bogart and Ida Lupino, the story had been remade as *Colorado Territory*, a Western with Joel McCrea and Virginia Mayo in 1949, then again as a modern gangster movie, *I Died a Thousand Times*, in 1955 with Jack Palance and Shelley Winters.

Many people believe that Al Capone inspired the central character in *Little Caesar*, but according to Burnett, that is not true. His inspirations for the novel were the small-time hoodlums and hobos he met when, as a young man, he worked as a desk clerk in one of Chicago's seedier hotels.

Because of his eyesight, Burnett had stopped writing by the time I interviewed him, and he was now spending his days promoting his still in-print novels, like *Little Caesar*, *High Sierra* and *The Asphalt Jungle*. He also expressed a concern that, unless copyright laws were changed, *Little Caesar* might soon enter the public domain, which would mean that his royalties from that book would cease.

We also discussed that night the problem with "handshake deals," and why he always insisted that all deals be in writing. "Even if everybody is being totally honest and above board with each other," he said, "you never know about 'the big black truck'."

"The big black truck?" I asked.

"One party to the deal steps off the sidewalk just as a big black truck barrels around the corner and runs him down," he said. "What happens to your deal then?"

Who but the premier writer of gangster fiction would deliver that bit of practical business advice in such a colorful manner?

The hours that I spent with William Riley Burnett that night are ones that I will always cherish.

One often gets valuable advice from a veteran writer. I don't recall the specific occasion, but I was in a restaurant with some actors, following the performance of an Equity waiver play they'd been in, and seated next to me was John Ball. He was the novelist who had created "Virgil Tibbs," the character played by Sidney Poitier in the Oscar-winning movie, *In the Heat of the Night*, plus two sequels.

Ball had written a series of popular mystery novels featuring the African-American police detective, but he was unhappy with the deal that was made for the film rights to *In the Heat of the Night*. In fact, he told me that he had fired his literary agent because of it.

According to Ball, as part of the deal, the film production company had acquired the dramatic rights to not only the original novel, but also to the character of "Virgil Tibbs". That meant that without further negotiations with Ball and for little or no future financial compensation to him, the producers could make as many sequels to *In the Heat of the Night* as they wished.

My knowledge of that deal is limited to what Ball told me that night. I was only hearing his side of the story; therefore there may well be other factors involved of which I'm not aware.

But, whatever the actual facts of Ball's predicament might have been, the lesson I learned that night was a valuable one for any writer, particularly one who is not a member of the Writer's Guild. Whenever you sell a screenplay, stage play or the dramatic rights to a novel or short story, make sure that your contract has provisions for possible sequels and remakes. Otherwise, you could be giving up some lucrative ancillary rights to your work.

Of course, if you're working as a "writer for hire," any character that you create belongs to your employer, though under WGA rules, you may get residual payments if they are reused. I recall talking to a writer who had written an episode of the old Don Adams series, *Get Smart*, for which he'd created a character, "Harry Hoo," played by Joey Forman, who was a "funny Charlie Chan".

This writer liked his Harry Hoo character so much that he thought of building a new television series around him, but then he realized that since he had introduced him in a *Get Smart* episode, the character actually belonged to the owners of that show.

Bummer!

Christopher Isherwood, Henry Ephron, Meredith Willson and Tennessee Williams were other extraordinary writers with whom I became acquainted during my years in Hollywood. I met Christopher Isherwood (*The Berlin Stories*, which later served as the basis for *Cabaret*), Oscar-winning actress Beatrice Straight (*Network*) and other notables at various gatherings at the Benedict Canyon home of client Nina Foch and her then husband, producer Michael Dewell, who founded the National Repertory Theater. Playwright Jerome Lawrence (*Inherit the Wind*), with whom I'd bumped heads a few years earlier over our competing books about Paul Muni, was also at those parties, but he made a point of avoiding me.

Playwright (with wife Phoebe) and producer Henry Ephron was a guest at the Motion Picture Home when I did volunteer work there. Though he was suffering from Alzheimer's, he was totally lucid during our weekly visits, and he relished in telling this captive listener stories about his years in show business. In particular, he liked to recount the reasons why Frank Sinatra quit the 1956 movie version of Rodgers and Hammerstein's *Carousel* (to be replaced by Gordon MacRae), which Ephron had produced.

Sinatra always claimed that he walked away when he learned that all scenes for the movie would have to be shot twice, once for the CinemaScope camera, then again for the new CinemaScope 55 process. "You're not getting two Sinatras for the price of one," he said.

Ephron, on the other hand, told me that he sensed that the singer was "afraid of the material; that he couldn't tackle it," and he used the dual cameras as his excuse for exiting the project.

I was including a chapter about *The Music Man* in my book, *The Musical: From Broadway to Hollywood*, which is why I phoned the office of its author/composer, Meredith Willson. His secretary informed me that her employer would be happy to cooperate, but that all questions had to be submitted to him "in writing," which is what I did.

A week or two later, I received a one-page letter from Willson's office that answered my questions, but did not elaborate with any unique insights into either the Broadway play or the movie that I could not have obtained without his help from previously published articles. Most troubling was the final line of the letter, which said something like "Mr. Willson insists that he read and approve your chapter before it is published."

I was not planning to say anything negative about the play or the movie in my book, but as a matter of principle, that was not going to happen. I was not about to give anybody the right to approve or disapprove my Work.

Willson's office was adamant. They demanded that they see the chapter before it was published. I was also adamant in my position, and this standoff went on for several months.

Finally, I offered a compromise. I would allow Willson to read the chapter and correct any factual errors, but my opinions would remain untouched. They, more or less, agreed to that proposal, and a few days later, I received a personal phone call from Meredith Willson, who sounded like he was reading a statement he had written: "Excellent chapter. I approve. Good luck."

About a month later, I met Willson face-to-face at an ASCAP event that was honoring my client, lyricist Paul Francis Webster. I would describe him as being "cordially reserved".

Certainly the most colorful of these writers was Tennessee Williams, arguably the greatest American playwright of the 20th century. In the latter part of the 1970s, I was hired to handle publicity for a local production of one of his lesser-known works, *The Two Character Play*. Directed by John Hancock (*Bang the Drum Slowly*), it starred Scott Wilson (*In Cold Blood*) and Hancock's wife, my then client, Dorothy Tristan (*Klute*, *Scarecrow*), with incidental music provided by future client, Oscar-winner Fred Karlin (*Lovers and Other Strangers*).

Having Tennessee Williams in town for this production was a publicist's dream. All I had to do was put out the word to the press that he was available and my phone started ringing.

Unfortunately, Hancock and his co-producer did not have it so easy with Williams, who not only had a major drinking problem, but he also wanted to leave Los Angeles for San Francisco where he hoped to get laid. So, in order to get Tennessee to stay and do necessary rewrites for the play, they hired him a handsome, young "driver" to chauffeur him around town and keep him happy.

That didn't work out. The "driver" had a hotel room that adjoined Williams' room, but he kept the connecting door locked. "The boy won't put out," Tennessee complained to Hancock.

In the past, Hancock had had a good working relationship with the playwright. He'd directed productions of *The Glass Menagerie*, *A Streetcar Named Desire* and *The Milk Train Doesn't Stop Here Anymore*. They both knew, going in, that *The Two Character Play* had structural issues, but Hancock, a master at "cutting, pasting and transposing" the parts of new plays into a cohesive whole, knew that if Williams would just knuckle down and work with him on the rewrite, they could come up with a viable piece of theatre.

I wasn't present on the night the two of them almost came to blows, but Hancock, who had hired me for this assignment, did recount to me what happened when he asked Williams to watch a run-through of the first act.

Apparently, Tennessee showed up exceedingly intoxicated, and after the actors had finished the run-through, he stood up and screamed, "I will denounce this as a violation of my play!"

When Hancock asked him what he didn't like, Williams told him that the most important scene in the play was gone.

"That scene comes in the second act," Hancock tried to explain, but Williams, in his drunken state, would not listen, and he continued to hurl insults at the director, who eventually lost all patience with Tennessee and called him a "phony cocksucker".

Williams stood his ground. "I have never been called that," he said.

Yelling and shouting continued on both sides until Williams made the mistake of insulting Tristan, Hancock's wife, with: "You look like Angie Dickinson on a bad night."

That did it. Hancock shouted, "The production is cancelled! Get the hell out of here!" Then, he chased Williams out of the theater and down the street.

Next morning, Hancock received a phone call from Williams' agent, who told him that the playwright was mortified by what he had done, and would Hancock please come over to his hotel so he could apologize.

Hancock went to the hotel where he found Williams working at his typewriter on the rewrites, a mug half coffee/half booze on the desk next to him. The apology was given, accepted and the play opened.

That opening night was rather special. The 99-seat theater on Melrose Avenue was filled with celebrities, including Natalie Wood, Robert Wagner, Amy Irving and many others, but as I recall, the play closed after one or two weekends of performances.

Encountering and, in most instances, getting to chat with these illustrious writers, definitely encouraged my own dreams of becoming a professional storyteller. I had already had publishing successes writing about Hollywood, the movies and its personalities, and my one-person plays, like *Gable*, (Spencer) *Tracy* and (Al) *Jolson*, were also drawing large audiences whenever they were staged. But, what I really wanted to do was see my own *original* stories published and/or produced on the stage and screen, and that wasn't happening yet.

I wondered if they ever would be…particularly after a lady I'd been seeing exclusively for many months, quipped: "Well, miracles do happen."

That relationship ended shortly thereafter.

Around that same period, I was hired by Gene Perret, an Emmy-winning and longtime comedy writer for Bob Hope. He wanted me to publicize his new "How to" book on writing comedy. It was a short-term relationship, and Gene was pleased with the job I did for him.

After my work had ended, I asked Gene if, as a personal favor, he would read and critique a stage comedy I'd written, and he agreed.

Two weeks later, he returned the script with a note: "I enjoyed this very much. You can do this work."

You can imagine how that made me feel.

With client Ned Wertimer, who played "Ralph," the doorman, on *The Jeffersons*, and my son, David, at his bar mitzvah reception.

With comedian/client Rip Taylor, in full make-up for his role of "Sheldon, the sea genie," on *Sigmund and the Sea Monsters*. When the *Sigmund* sound stage at the Goldwyn Studio burned to the ground, Rip had to return to his hotel that night in that outfit. *[Sorry for the poor quality of this Polaroid shot.]*

My former client, Lynn Borden (*Hazel*, *Frogs*) and her husband, Roger Brunelle, at one of my book signings.

Steve Kanaly has just learned that he has become a victim on *TV Bloopers and Practical Jokes*.

Photo Section • 151

Abe Vigoda was another client I set up for *TV Bloopers and Practical Jokes*. The "cop" eyeing me is actor Lee Ryan.

Chatting with actor/producer Sheldon Leonard. At that time, he was considering doing an *I Spy* reunion TV movie with Bill Cosby and Robert Culp. "I will only do it if there are *no problems*," he said. "I don't want *any* problems."

Clint Howard had roles in both *Cheyenne Warrior* and *Dillinger and Capone*. This photo was taken at Texas Frightmare Weekend (2012) in Dallas.

Like with Broderick Crawford, Kevin McCarthy was an actor who I pursued, but was never able to sign as a publicity client. Yet, we always had a friendly relationship. He was a bit taken aback at this autograph show when I showed him a program from the London production of *Death of a Salesman*, in which he'd appeared with Paul Muni. I had purchased the Muni-autographed item on ebay and Kevin was happy to add his signature to the piece, which is now framed and hanging on my wall.

Photo Section • 153

You meet the nicest people at autograph shows, like Oscar-winning actress, Celeste Holm.

You also get reacquainted with old friends at autograph shows, like Dawn Wells (*Gilligan's Island*), who was a student at the University of Washington Drama Department at the same time that I was there.

Lovely June Wilkinson, who had a major role in *Keaton's Cop*, a film we would both like to forget, came to the Los Angeles book signing for *My Forty-Five Years in Hollywood...And How I Escaped Alive*.

Don Maloney, Roy Scheider, Christian Harmony and Teresa DePriest in a scene from *The Doorway*.

I was interviewed for a retrospective featurette that was part of *The Maltese Falcon* "Special Edition" DVD, released by Warner Home Video.

Sandy and me in London at Buckingham Palace.

With my friend, Bruce Kimmel, at a Chicago autograph show.
Bruce worked with me on the musical version of *Hail on the Chief!*

These beautiful ladies played various roles in the first staged reading of *Hail on the Chief!* From left: Pamela Taylor, Lisa Robert, my longtime dear friend, Bridget Hanley, and Stephnie Renz.

I don't know the identity of the "fan" in the center of this picture, but that's me with Dan O'Herlihy at an autograph show.

I'm standing in the Chicago alley (down the street from the Biograph Theater) in which the FBI killed John Dillinger in 1934. Gangster buff that I am, it's the first place I visited when I came to the "Windy City" in 2010 to appear at an autograph show.

Surrounded by "Bond Girls" Britt Ekland, Maud Adams and Lana Wood at the 2010 autograph show in Chicago.

The delightful Ruth Buzzi and I were seated next to each other at the 2010 autograph show in Chicago. Wife Sandy was out of the room when we took this picture.

That's my Austin next-door neighbor, Scott Whitaker, and me at the 2011 Wizard World Comic Con.

Me with another "Michael" at Texas Frightmare Weekend (2012).

Me with the amiable Clu Gulager at Son of Monsterpalooza in Burbank (2012).

Kate was my wonderful dog for twelve years, but she certainly didn't know how to deal with Charlie, a pain-in the-ass parrot who briefly shared our condo. I quickly found Charlie a new owner after I spread the word that, if somebody didn't take him, I would not have to buy a turkey for Thanksgiving. Sorry, but I guess I'm not a bird person.

Jasmine and Missy: A love affair?

Missy and Annie were both with me for almost seventeen years. At first, they did not get along, but they, eventually, became good buddies. I miss them both, as well as Jasmine, who was also with me for many years.

My new best friend, Chester.

My handsome son, David. I am proud of him.

Sandy and me. She is the love of my life.

In the late spring of 2013, the Fort Wayne Civic Theatre staged a production of my play, *Lombard*, which gave me the opportunity to visit Carole Lombard's childhood home. She was born in Fort Wayne and lived in this house until her mother and brothers moved to Los Angeles when she was eight.

Psst! Wanna buy a book? Have pen. Will sign.

18

Writing & Roger Corman

WRITING BOOKS AND PLAYS about the Golden Age of Hollywood and its iconic stars was a joyful experience for me. The actual writing part was "work"; the pleasure was in meeting and interviewing the people from that time who were still around in the 1970s and 80s, but have since gone to that great movie studio up in the sky.

Henry Blanke was one of them. A longtime contract producer at Warner Brothers, his credits include classics like *The Adventures of Robin Hood*, *The Maltese Falcon* and *The Treasure of Sierra Madre*.

I met with Blanke on several occasions at his home for interviews on different books. I always sensed bitterness about him, but we never discussed the reasons for his occasional outbursts, and I assumed that he was experiencing early dementia. However, that didn't prevent him from sharing some juicy stories with me, including one involving a drunk and unconscious Errol Flynn being dumped one night on the lawn of his frequent co-star, Basil Rathbone.

The screen's greatest swashbuckler had attended one of the Rathbone's lavish parties the day before, had followed a lady home and, after a few too many drinks, he had passed out in her living room. Late that night, she and a friend had "returned" him to the Rathbones.

The next morning, Basil and his wife, Ouida, were having breakfast on their patio when the gardener turned on the sprinklers. The Rathbones, mouths agape, watched their friend spring up from the grass, bid them "Good morning," and depart.

I had done a phone interview with director William A. Wellman (*The Public Enemy*, *Beau Geste*, *The Ox-Bow Incident*), but I didn't meet him in person until a few months later when we were both booked, along with actress Leslie Caron (*Gigi*), to appear on a local television interview show. Like me, he was promoting his new book.

It's customary on shows of this ilk for the guest or his publicist to supply the producers with a promotion copy of the book, so that the interviewer can read it in advance and also display it for the camera. They, after all, are giving the author free airtime and publicity that will, hopefully, help sell the book.

However, after his interview was over, crusty "Wild Bill" Wellman did something I'd never seen in all my years as a publicist. He snatched his book back from the rather surprised host, who asked, "Can't I keep it?"

"No," Wellman said. "You can buy a copy." Then, he left the television studio.

Some of the people I interviewed astonished me with their candidness. Jose Ferrer (an Oscar winner for *Cyrano de Bergerac*), for example, divulged that "no director in town wanted to touch *Return to Peyton Place*," and that he took the job because he "wasn't much in demand as a director then, and he needed the credit." Sadly, that sequel to its hit predecessor was a flop both critically and financially. "I wish I had had, at least, one successful film during my directing career," Ferrer admitted.

On the other hand, when I interviewed her at the Beverly Hills Brown Derby, Yvonne de Carlo (*The Munsters*) didn't really want to talk about the topic at hand. All she wanted to discuss was her sex life and the men she'd slept with, including Howard Hughes.

Without doubt, the most shocking revelation I ever heard in an interview came from Jet Fore, a veteran publicist who worked for years at 20th Century-Fox. Jet was a very straightforward guy, thus I have no reason to believe what he told me was not true. Nevertheless, since he is no longer with us and I have never been able to verify this story with a second source, I'm not going to reveal the names of the people involved.

According to Jet, two actors under contract to Fox, one a major star and the other a well known character actor, got drunk one night and were driving in Malibu when their car struck and killed a woman who was walking along the side of the road. Jet was called in the middle of the night to help insure that the tragic accident was never reported in the press, which, apparently, it wasn't.

Fox and the other major studios certainly had a lot of power back in the day.

Jet was one of the most likable publicists in the business, and he was always helpful to me. When I was working on *Make It Again, Sam*, my book about movie remakes, the Richard Lester version of *The Three Musketeers* was two or three months away from its release date, so Jet was kind enough to set up a special screening of the film for me at the studio. We were the only two people in the screening room that day, and while I watched the movie, he sat in the row behind me, snoring away.

At the beginning of the 1980s, the interview sources for the kind of film-oriented books that I was writing were becoming scarce. True, a lot of these people were passing away, but the survivors were getting wary of the authors who were interviewing them. Director Gordon Douglas (*Tony Rome, Them!*), for instance, had given me an ingenuous interview about his 1966 remake of *Stagecoach* for *Make It Again, Sam*, but he refused to talk to me a few months later when I called him for comments for my next book. "I don't do interviews anymore," he told me.

Douglas' coolness baffled me. I knew he couldn't be upset with me, because *Make It Again, Sam* had not even been published yet.

The problem, as I would soon discover, was that some of my writing colleagues were starting to come out with Hollywood-oriented books, mostly unauthorized biographies, that scandalized their subjects with questionable accusations and innuendoes, and the friends of these deceased personalities did not want to contribute to this muck.

One of the earliest, and perhaps the most sensational of these celebrity "biographies," was a book by the late Charles Higham that accused Errol Flynn of spying for the Nazis during World War II, a claim that virtually everybody who knew the deceased actor vehemently denied.

I knew Higham; had lunched with him a couple of times, but I could never really warm up to him or his questionable ethics as a Hollywood biographer and historian. He looked for vicious gossip lurking in the pasts of his dead subjects, and if he couldn't find a real scandal, he would create one using faulty deductions in lieu of actual evidence. He would justify these dubious assertions with statements like: "So-and-so told me this before he died."

[I realize that, a few paragraphs earlier, I did something similar to this when I related what Jet Fore had told me. The difference is that I knew my source to be a viable one but more importantly, unlike with Higham, I didn't reveal the identities of the people involved, so nobody's reputation was tarnished.]

A few years after Higham's book was published, I met one of Flynn's daughters at a party in Hollywood. She told me that the family had sued Higham over his claims, but the court had not only dismissed the case, but had also made the Flynn family pay Higham's legal fees. It seems that, under the law, you cannot libel or slander a dead person.

One of the perks in writing books about Hollywood is that you suddenly become an acknowledged "expert" in the field, and you're asked to write columns, as I did monthly for over a year for *Coronet Magazine*, or to appear on television shows like *Merv Griffin* and *Entertainment Tonight*, which was doing a segment on the Hollywood musical. The producer of that story had read my book, *The Musical: From Broadway to Hollywood*.[1]

In later years, the folks at Warner Home Video interviewed me on-camera for the special featurettes they shot that were included in their DVD releases of vintage films, like *The Maltese Falcon* and *A Slight Case of Murder*.

I may have been having fun writing my movie books and enjoying my "Hollywood historian" status, but that wasn't satisfying whatever "artist" in me actually existed. The screenplays I'd been writing had not been selling and none of my stage plays had ever been produced, although one of them had had a promising staged reading in front of a full audience at actor Lonny Chapman's esteemed Group Repertory Theatre, and another was read at the Melrose Theatre in Hollywood. Neither of those readings resulted in a full production.

My writing situation took a definite upturn when I started turning out one-person plays about Hollywood's great movie stars, starting with Clark Gable, then relatively quickly followed by Spencer Tracy, Carole Lombard, Al Jolson, Orson Welles and others.

Artistically, I still wasn't telling my own original stories, but I was now able to mold these biographies into a dramatic structure and, even more satisfying, though they were based on real people, I was creating breathing characters and dealing with their deepest emotions.

From a commercial standpoint, the advantage to doing these two act monologues was that you didn't have to sell them to the public. All one

---

1. Watching that *ET* segment was a definite high. Beside myself, the other "authorities" interviewed included Gene Kelly, Norman Jewison, Tim Rice and Joseph Papp.

had to really do was to let it be known that a Clark Gable or Spencer Tracy play was being presented, and their fans would fill the Equity Waiver theater every night.

I made it a point to attend most performances of my plays, and I would often hear audience members during the show whispering among themselves with comments like, "I remember when he did that…."

The late Sid Conrad, the magnificent actor who starred in my play, *Tracy*, once said to me: "The good thing about being in a one-person play is that you get mentioned in the reviews. The bad thing is that the cast parties are pretty lonely."

At the end of the 1980s, I finally sold a screenplay, *Keaton's Cop*, which starred Lee Majors, Abe Vigoda, Don Rickles and June Wilkinson, and it was a total disaster. It is a terrible movie that bears scant relation to my original script and, for a time, I thought that my screenwriting career would be over before it even began.

The *good news* is that I've made more money from *Keaton's Cop* residuals than the movie grossed in theaters and, as I write this chapter twenty-two years after the picture's release, I am still receiving residual checks…as recently as yesterday.

The fact was that, good or bad, with *Keaton's Cop*, I now had a "hard credit," which eventually resulted in my selling two of my other original screenplays, *Big Al and Desperate Dan* (produced as *Dillinger and Capone*) and *Cheyenne Warrior* to Roger Corman, who later hired me to write many other screenplays for him, including *The Doorway* starring Roy Scheider, which I also directed at his studio in Ireland.

All of these projects are discussed at length in my first memoir, so, once again:

READ THE OTHER BOOK!

As I said in that earlier volume, I may have learned to write more efficiently working for Roger Corman, but I don't think that any of the scripts I wrote for him were as good (or heartfelt) as the ones that I wrote for myself on spec. Of course, the advantage of writing for Roger was that I always got paid and, in most instances, the resulting screenplay, in one form or another, was produced.

With the exception of *Cheyenne Warrior*, I may not have been happy with the finished product, but that's beside the point.

Most of my dissatisfaction stemmed from the fact that my approach to the art of storytelling is different from Roger's. In a Corman script, characterization is secondary to action and, almost always, the movie starts out with some sort of "shocking" scene that will grab and hold the audience until the next "shocking" scene that occurs ten or fifteen minutes into the picture.

Conversely, I believe that, in order for an audience to care about what happens to a character during that initial "shocking" moment, they need to know that character somewhat, which is why I prefer a more gradual development of a story. The viewer, after all, has either purchased a theater ticket, bought or rented a DVD or has paid to have a movie streamed into their home, so he is not going to stop watching it if the world doesn't blow up or a Tyrannosaurus Rex doesn't appear on screen and devour a half nude beauty within the first fifteen minutes.

Alfred Hitchcock was a master at letting his films unfold slowly. If you don't believe me, just take a look at some of his most revered thrillers (e.g. *Rear Window*, *The Man Who Knew Too Much*, *Psycho*, *The Birds*), and you'll see that nothing *really* significant happens for the first fifteen minutes or so of any of those classics. That's because, before he "shocked" his audience, he wanted them to "bond" with his characters.

Every writer needs a good story editor, and I had two excellent ones when I wrote for Roger, Beverly Gray and Frances Doel.

With Beverly, we sat together and read aloud my drafts of *Dillinger and Capone*, and as we did that, it became perfectly apparent to me which lines of dialogue worked and which ones were unnecessary.

Frances, on the other hand, would give me several pages of notes for each draft, and if there were something in the script that she didn't like, she would suggest one or two ways to correct it. I may not have always gone along with her specific ideas, but even when I discarded them, they encouraged me to rethink the troubling dialogue or scene so that I would eventually come up with a better solution to the problem.

Corman's policy with writers was that, whenever a new draft of a script was submitted, it would be passed around to several people, including interns, in the company, who would be required to read it and submit notes.

I didn't like that practice. Indeed, I have never been a believer in "writer's groups" where people meet, read and critique each other's manuscripts. If ten writers are critiquing one manuscript, that's going to result in ten different opinions, and good writing is never accomplished by a "committee".

As I said, every writer needs a good, qualified story editor; one who will be totally honest with them and whose opinion they trust. When I worked for Corman, I told Frances Doel that I didn't want to read the notes from others in the office. Instead, I wanted her to read them, and then submit to me only the ones she thought were valid. Indeed, some of the notes submitted by interns were useless; had nothing to do with story, character or dialogue but, for example, dealt with the choreography of a gunfight that the film's director would deal with on the set.

What the hell did I care if an actor turned right or left when he fired his rifle?

Having Frances filter the notes before I saw them worked extremely well.

When Roger gave me the opportunity in 1999 to direct my screenplay of *The Doorway*, a horror/black comedy dealing with demons from Hell, he did throw some unexpected challenges at me, but I'm told that he often did that with his directors.

About two weeks before we began filming at his studio in Ireland, I was informed by Robert Hall, my make-up special effects artist, that instead of my well-researched concept of mythological demons I had planned for the movie, the budget that Roger had given him would only allow for demons in spandex body suits and pullover Halloween masks.

That was certainly disappointing, but I figured that I could still shoot the picture in such a way that it would be easy to edit in pick-up shots once Roger saw how terrible these spandex demons looked on screen… which is what happened during post-production in Los Angeles.

A week later, I was told that *The Doorway*, originally set to be recorded with a Hi-Def camera, was now going to be shot on 35mm. Hi-Def was a relatively new process then, and I can only assume that, with Roy Scheider having been signed to star, Roger felt that selling this picture on a film format would be easier, particularly in foreign markets.[2]

Finally, about two days before shooting was to start, I was told that the budget did not allocate funds for my cinematographer, Yoram Astrakhan, to have either a dolly or a wide-angle lens. "You have what you have," Roger responded when I objected during that phone conversation.

---

2. When casting *The Doorway*, I had been given a choice between Charlton Heston and Roy Scheider as my star. I picked Scheider because, not only did I think he was the better actor, but because I had written a book about Heston in 1976 that was not entirely complimentary, and I figured that, if he recognized my name, that could cause problems during production.

We did, nevertheless, get the dolly and the lens. Yoram went to John, the movie's line producer in Ireland, and agreed to shoot less film stock than had been budgeted for in exchange for those two indispensable items. That's why, once filming began, Yoram would get upset with me if I took too long to call "Action" after the camera had started rolling. "Film stock is wasting," he would say.

"Good," I quipped once. "I own shares in Eastman Kodak."

One of the other production challenges I had to deal with on *The Doorway* had nothing to do with Roger or the film's budget. It had to do with a prop.

A leading character in the movie is an aspiring actor. His hero is W.C. Fields, who he mimics at various times throughout the film. If his mimicking was to make sense, for one scene I needed a photograph or drawing of the classic comedian, which the actor would hang on the wall.

I chose a W.C. Fields poster that cost about five dollars from a New York movie memorabilia dealer's catalog. Corman's office in Los Angeles was to order it and have it shipped via Fed-Ex to me at the studio in Ireland. Since the scene in which the poster appeared was not going to be shot until the second week of filming, they had a total of four weeks (including three weeks of pre-production) to accomplish this simple task.

I don't know why the poster never arrived. Even with my daily phone calls to Corman's office during the first week of shooting to remind them that time was running short, it didn't show up. I was told that the memorabilia dealer screwed up, so perhaps it might be wise for me to just do some rewriting, and not mention W.C. Fields at all.

I guess they didn't know me very well. A missing prop was not going to back me into a corner; force me to not only rewrite several scenes, but also re-shoot other scenes in which the W.C. Fields references had already been established.

The day before the scene in question was to be shot, I had one of the Irish production assistants download a rough pen-and-ink drawing of Fields from the Internet. He enlarged it, and then since he was also a gifted artist, he spruced it up, tea-stained it and put the finished image into a frame.

We shot the scene with this improvised prop, and it actually worked pretty well in the finished picture.

Despite some of the conditions under which I had to write…and direct…I have nothing but the highest regard for Roger Corman. Without him, many of my show business dreams might not have ever come true. I appreciate the many opportunities he afforded me; the respect he has always shown for my talents.

I am proud to be an alumnus of the Corman School of Filmmaking.

19

The Ambush

NOT EVERY PROJECT TURNS OUT the way a writer would like.

Sometimes a script works and sometimes it doesn't.

I've had my fair share of disappointments, as well as my fair share of successes. That's the nature of the business I've chosen.

It's not unusual for a good screenplay, once it's in the hands of the producer, director and actors, to go through such drastic changes that the finished movie bears scant resemblance to what the original writer envisioned.

I've heard of actors who will adjust a line or two of dialogue and then claim that they've "saved the picture."

These interpretive artists are not trying to destroy the work. They honestly think that they are improving it, and often they do.

And, often they don't.

Whatever the outcome, it's seldom that these creative people deliberately try to sabotage a project. That can hurt everybody involved…unless the saboteur has an ulterior motive.

In 1999, a few months before I went to Ireland to direct *The Doorway* for Roger Corman, a somewhat well known variety performer threw a monkey wrench into one of my potentially lucrative stage projects, stopping it dead in its tracks. Personally, I think it was a deliberate "assassination," but I'm going to let you read the facts and decide for yourself.

I'm also not going to tell you his name. Why should I give him the publicity? So, we'll call him "Ollie".

The most successful of my one-person plays was *Jolson*, in part because it was a musical with a score that consisted of songs Al Jolson made famous, "April Showers," "Swanee," "My Mammy" and so forth. It did so well that I decided to do another one-person "juke box musical," this one about the great French entertainer, Maurice Chevalier, whose song hits included "Louise" and "Thank Heaven for Little Girls" from *Gigi*.

When I wrote *Chevalier*, I did something I had not done in my seven previous one-person plays. I did not include flashbacks. Chevalier's entire two-act monologue, as well as the songs he sang, was set in the present. I was pleased with the finished result.

Obtaining licenses to incorporate the songs I needed for my show, however, was not an easy matter. Unlike when I had requested the songs for *Jolson* a decade earlier, copyright holders were no longer willing to give me a favored nations agreement or an open ended license for their songs. In fact, each publisher seemed to want something different.

The negotiations became so convoluted that, when Frances Doel called me from Roger Corman's office with an offer to write them another screenplay, I took the job and put *Chevalier* on the shelf, figuring that I could revisit the licensing negotiations sometime in the future.

Awhile later, I received a phone call from Hy Juter, a New York producer who was interested in my Al Jolson play. Since I was then in negotiations with another producer who wanted to stage *Jolson* off-Broadway (a deal that, eventually, fell through), I informed Juter that the show was not available, but then I told him about *Chevalier*.

He liked the idea of a one-person musical about Maurice Chevalier and asked me to send him the script, which I did. I figured that if Juter decided to produce the play, he would deal with the various copyright holders with regard to the needed song licenses.

A week or two later, Juter told me that he wanted to produce *Chevalier*. In fact, he was setting up a "backer's audition" at a small theater in New York City, and he was going to pay my air fare, hotel and other out-of-pocket expenses for me to come East and participate in the reading.

He also told me that he had set Ollie to play Chevalier for the reading, which I thought was a great choice because Ollie was a "name" that would help draw an audience to the event.

We both knew that, since this was a first draft of the play, revisions would have to be made, but I also informed him that before I agreed as to exactly *what* had to be changed, I needed to hear my script read aloud and also see an audience's reaction to the material.

I have never been one of those writers who believe that every word I write is sacred. If I see that a line or a scene is not working, I will be the first one to insist that it be changed or cut altogether. Watching a dress rehearsal for the initial production of *Jolson*, for instance, I suddenly realized that a particular scene was unnecessary and slowing the forward progression of the play. At the end of that rehearsal, I told the director to cut the scene, which she did, and the play was better without it.

One of the advantages of being a playwright, as opposed to a screenwriter, is that you have total control over the words in your play. Nobody can make a change in the script without your permission. That doesn't mean that you shouldn't listen to suggestions from people whose opinions you trust. But, before you make any revisions, you must believe that those changes will, indeed, give you a better play.

At the end of the day, that's *your* name on the script.

I flew into New York the night before the first of two scheduled rehearsals. Juter picked me up at JFK, took me to dinner then dropped me off at my hotel, which faced Central Park. I liked him immediately, an agreeable, generous man.

It may have been after ten o'clock in New York, but my body was still on Los Angeles time. I couldn't sleep, so after I'd dropped my suitcase off in my room, I decided to go for a walk.

Sharing the elevator with me as I descended to the lobby was a gorgeous, well dressed blonde. "Are you from the West Coast, too?" I asked, trying to be friendly. "Can't sleep?"

"Actually," she smiled, " I'm a 'working girl'. It's $200 for a blow-job."

I passed, as I did with the redhead who approached me as I emerged from the hotel to ask if I "wanted a date."

New York had not changed since my last visit. The hookers were still out in force…even in the upper end areas.

But that night wasn't anywhere as memorable as my first trip to New York in 1973. I was there then on behalf of a publicity client, and to meet with the publisher of my first book.

Not only was the city overflowing with hookers in 1973, but it also seemed like everybody and his brother was getting mugged. A few months earlier, my friend, columnist James Bacon, was robbed at knifepoint right in front of his hotel.

I'm not kidding when I tell you that I was totally paranoid when I got off the plane. I actually half expected the baggage handler to mug me. To make matters worse, I had the world's nastiest cab driver take me into town. He didn't like the five-dollar tip I gave him, and he started swearing at me in front of my hotel.

I was so fearful that when Jack Tierman, a New York publicist with whom I sometimes collaborated, invited me to see a film he was promoting at a screening room two blocks from my hotel, I agreed to go…providing that he walk me back to the hotel after it had ended.

Jack did, in fact, escort me around much of the Broadway area that night, after which I felt quite comfortable strolling about on my own. I just made it a point to stay on crowded, well-lit streets.

Returning to 1999: The day after I arrived in New York, I wandered up and down Broadway until it was time for the rehearsal to start, then walked over to the theater. Juter, Ollie, the director, Stephen Demeno, and a pianist were already there. Everybody seemed to be pretty amiable.

The rehearsal itself went well. Ollie sold the songs, and for the purpose of a staged reading, his presentation of my script may not have been anything that Robert DeNiro or Laurence Olivier would have to worry about, but it was definitely acceptable. He readily incorporated the few suggestions that Demeno and I gave to him that afternoon into his performance.

We had a second rehearsal the next afternoon before the reading that evening. Demeno and I were pleased when we broke for dinner. We both felt that we were going to have a good show.

Were we in for a surprise….

The theater that night was filled. Hy Juter had done his job well. Representatives of the Gershwin Estate were present, as well as other potential backers for the show.

I had invited some of my own New York friends, including former client, actor George Dickerson, who is probably best remembered for his role as Laura Dern's police detective father in David Lynch's *Blue Velvet* (1986). George and his charming wife, Suzanne, have lived for years in an apartment on the top floor (no elevator) of a five story building in Greenwich Village that used to be occupied by revered film critic and screenwriter James Agee (*The African Queen, The Night of the Hunter*). George claims that Agee's ghost, with whom he has conversed, haunts the apartment.

The lights went down. The performance began with Ollie doing a fine rendition of the opening number, "Thank Heaven for Little Girls." Applause. Applause.

Then, he started to read the monologue…and did he *READ* it.

There was no inflection. No attempt to suggest the character of Maurice Chevalier. He delivered my words in the dullest monotone that I have ever heard, like a marble statue reading the phone book.

Demeno and I looked at each other. We were both thinking the same thing: "What the hell is going on here?" [Actually, the word that came to my mind was not "hell".]

When Ollie got to the next song, "Sweepin' the Clouds Away," he delivered it beautifully, pure Chevalier. Then, it was back to my script and the somnambulist reading. That's the way it went for the entire performance, a great delivery of the songs, but no effort whatsoever to instill any life into my words.

I could only think of two logical explanations for Ollie's behavior. Either he'd "frozen" when it came time for him to perform my script, forgetting everything that we'd accomplished in the rehearsals, or he had deliberately sabotaged the performance.

The first possibility didn't make sense. This man was a show business veteran, well known for his television and nightclub appearances. Even if he was not an accomplished "actor," he certainly possessed enough professional experience and charm to give my script, at the very least, a decent reading.

And, if it were his clandestine intent all along to see my script fail, then the big question would be: *"Why?"*

It would be several months before I learned the answer.

In the meantime, once Ollie's inexplicable performance had ended that night, I, as the playwright, had to take part in a Q&A with the audience; perhaps the most humiliating experience of my life.

I cannot express how angry, depressed and frustrated I was during that twenty-minute session. I couldn't say what I was really thinking, that Ollie was a first-rate jerk, because that would come off as sour grapes. No, I had to sit there, smile and answer the audience's questions, which were surprisingly gentle and polite.

Actually, despite Ollie's non-performance of my script, several moments had still registered with these folks and had elicited laughs.

When the event was over and the people had left, my friend, George Dickerson, said to me, "You realize that you were 'ambushed' tonight, don't you?"

"Yes," I said, "I'm still in shock."

Since I had an eight o'clock flight back to Los Angeles the next morning, Hy Juter had booked a hotel room for me close to JFK. It was around midnight when I took a cab out to the airport, but I was still so upset that I knew I was not going to be able to sleep. Instead, I figured I'd just go straight to JFK and sit in the terminal.

That was a stupid thing to do.

That terminal was totally deserted. Maybe there was a janitor or a security guard someplace, but I never saw or heard them. I sat alone in that cavernous room for several hours, reading a book I had with me, but, for the most part, brooding.

I not only felt sorry for myself, I also felt badly for Hy Juter who had probably spent a few thousand dollars to finance the disastrous evening. That investment was not going to garner him any financial backers for my play.

I had been alone in the brightly lit terminal for three or four hours when a military serviceman joined me. Home on leave, he was also booked on the eight o'clock flight. He was a nice guy, good company; then an hour or so later, a young man, who frankly looked like he belonged to a gang, walked into the terminal and asked if either of us could change a fifty-dollar bill. We both shook our heads, and the guy left.

That's when I realized that my choosing to wait alone all night in an empty airport terminal was a stupid thing to do. I have no doubt that, had that serviceman not been with me, I would have been robbed that night or even worse.

A word to the wise....

I don't recall exactly how long it was after the New York reading, a few months or possibly even a year, that I read that Ollie was performing a Maurice Chevalier act in various venues around the country.

In my mind, that made everything that had happened crystal clear. If Ollie had been planning all along to do his own Chevalier show, then he would definitely want to limit the competition, and by destroying my play before it even had a chance to get started made perfect sense.

I certainly didn't have any exclusivity on doing a Maurice Chevalier project, but if Ollie was using my script...or any part of it...that would be copyright infringement.

My attorney sent Ollie a letter, which was answered shortly by his lawyer, who claimed that Ollie had never heard of me and didn't know what I was talking about. However, when my attorney offered to send them a copy of the program from the New York reading, Ollie's memory was suddenly refreshed, and he now claimed that his act incorporated absolutely nothing that I had written.

He was telling the truth. I saw his act a few years later on DVD and it was not at all like my play, *Chevalier*. It was a nightclub act, nothing more.

But, that's not the point.

What Ollie did to me (and Hy Juter) that night in New York was totally underhanded and despicable. *Chevalier* might very well have moved forward had it not been for his dreadful performance. Or, it might still have died there. We'll never really know.

Ollie's kind of backstabbing is done every day in the field of entertainment. They call it "business."

Remember what Tessio (Abe Vigoda) says in his final scene in *The Godfather* after his plot to assassinate Michael Corleone (Al Pacino) is uncovered?

"Tell Mike it was only business. I always liked 'im."

Isn't it wonderful to have friends and associates like that?

20

Pet Projects

AFTER I FINISHED *THE DOORWAY,* I continued to write off-and-on for Roger Corman. Some of those scripts were produced (e.g. *Raptor*), while others gather dust on the shelf (e.g. *Cheyenne Warrior II*).

At one point, there was even a brief possibility that I might become the chief story editor for either Roger or producer Elliott Kastner (*Where Eagles Dare, The Long Goodbye*), who was in negotiations to purchase Roger's company, Concorde-New Horizons. Had that deal actually been finalized, Roger might have been required to relinquish story editor Frances Doel's services to Kastner and, since at that time I was the most active (and expensive) writer turning out scripts for Corman, I was informed that I could be her likely replacement.

On the other hand, had Roger been able to keep Frances on his team, he had assured me that he would make a strong recommendation to Kastner that I be hired as Concorde-New Horizons' story editor.

I think I would have been good at that job. Story, three-act structure, character development and dialogue were second nature to me. Constructing individual plot points was more of a challenge, but, eventually, I would find a way to make all the elements fit together into a cohesive whole. I'd taught screenwriting at an adult university and my book, *The Art of Storytelling*, had been used as a text for college classes in various parts of the country.

Ultimately, however, when the Kastner deal fell apart, all of this talk became moot. Frances continued as Roger's story editor and I continued to write for him and others.

Some of the other scripts that I wrote, and occasionally still do write, were for people outside or on the fringes of show business. They have a story idea that they want turned into a screenplay, and my services have either been recommended to them by a mutual acquaintance, or they have read or seen something that I've written. If I like the story idea and am not currently working on another assignment, I will take on their project. I love to write...especially if I'm being paid to do it.

Since these folks can seldom afford my going rate, I will often make them a deal whereby they pay me "sit down money" to cover the time, usually 6-8 weeks, that it will take to write a good first draft, plus I will get writing credit and fifty percent ownership in the screenplay. To make sure that there are no misunderstandings, I also point out to these clients that, no matter how good my finished work might be, there is a 99% chance that this screenplay will never sell and that the upfront fee they pay me will be money that they will never recoup.

Also, after having an unfortunate misunderstanding with one of these writing clients several years ago, I now make it very clear that I am just writing a first draft of the script, and it will be solely their responsibility to sell it. The sad truth is that all work of this nature is speculative and marketability is dependent on the ever-changing whims of the entertainment industry.

As actor James Coburn (*The Great Escape*, *The President's Analyst*) once said: "Getting a movie made today is a miracle." I am not a worker of miracles.

Every writer has a pet project sitting on his shelf that, no matter how many times he tries to jump start it, never seems to be able to take off and fly on its own.

Actually, I have two. Both of them are stage plays.

You might say that the first one is autobiographical.

No matter how much they love their kids, every parent has to deal with them becoming a teenager and young adult. Not the easiest of tasks.

Let's be honest. Teenagers and young adults are pains in the *tuchis* for their parents, and my son, David, was no different.

I'm sure I made mistakes with him when he was younger, but I definitely paid for them during his years between fifteen and twenty-five.

In 1990, I decided to write a two-character stage play based on our relationship. I figured that, after writing so many one-person stage plays, it was time for me to graduate. The play, which I initially titled *Father and Son,* may have been a work of fiction, but the characters definitely mirrored our personalities and several incidents dramatized in the work had their basis in fact.

I wrote *Father and Son* with David's blessing and input. It is a comedy, sort of a cross between Woody Allen and Neil Simon in its style, and it turned out quite well.

Reni Santoni (*Enter Laughing*, *Dirty Harry*) read the play, loved it and agreed to play the father (me). With him on board, the owner of a popular Equity-waiver theater in the San Fernando Valley decided to produce the play with myself as director.

We cast the role of the son, and even started rehearsals, but less than a week into the process, the theater owner announced that he had received a lucrative offer to rent out his 99-seat house for another show. He would still let us perform the play on Tuesday and Wednesday nights, but without weekend performances or any meaningful rehearsal time in the theater, both Reni and I knew that garnering an audience would be difficult if not impossible, so the production was cancelled.

The script went onto the shelf, where it has remained. I did, however, change the title a few years back. It is now called *Putz*.

If is ever produced, I just wonder what they will use as a logo.

My other pet project is called *Hail on the Chief!*

The idea for this comedy first came to me back in the early 1980s when I was lunching at an outdoor Santa Barbara restaurant with my friend, Ed Siemens. Ed told me about a colleague of his whose young kids had accidentally wandered onto the back section of then-President Ronald Reagan's ranch and, within minutes, they were surrounded by a small army of Secret Service agents, weapons drawn, and helicopters flying overhead.

That anecdote got my creative juices working: What if you hated your next-door neighbor, who suddenly gets elected President of the United States? How would you deal with all the inconveniences that would naturally be imposed upon your life?

I pondered that premise for a time before I actually sat down and started to put something on paper, but when I did, I'd decided that *Hail on the Chief!* would be a seven character farce written for the stage.

My "hero," or protagonist, would be a curmudgeon, a former screenwriter who now creates games for a living. He lives on a small ranch, sharing an access road with a neighboring ranch belonging to a former cowboy movie star, sort of a fusion of Gene Autry and Ronald Reagan, who he hates because of an old property line dispute. This character never appears on stage, but as the play opens, he's just been elected President of the United States.

My hero's chief nemesis (i.e. the antagonist) is a veteran, somewhat paranoid Secret Service agent. He believes "if you didn't vote for the President, you have to be out to get him," which puts him into an escalating, almost slapstick game of dirty tricks and gotcha moments with the hero.

The play also needed a true "heavy"; an actual threat to the President-elect, which would, ultimately, motivate our hero to change his ways and put his country before his petty vendettas against his neighbor and the Secret Service agent. Since "Libyan hit squads," with Reagan as their target, were front-page news then, I gave serious consideration to that possibility, but I finally dropped the idea because they were *too* dangerously real. This, after all, was a comedy.

What I needed was a "comic heavy" who might have nefarious plans, but was a character that the audience would never believe was a serious threat to anybody. My inspiration came from the 1979 movie, *The In-Laws* with Peter Falk and Alan Arkin. Appearing only in the final half hour of that hilarious film, Richard Libertini played a mad South American dictator who was so loony that the audience could not stop laughing. Indeed, Libertini continues to crack me up every time I see *The In-Laws*.

My comic heavy was not from South America. He was the delusional self-appointed "king" of a small island in Micronesia with an evil plan to force the United States into financing a luxury gambling resort on his island that, unfortunately, had an extremely active volcano right in its center. As my hero quips: "I can see this is going to be a vacation spot for the high rollers."

I cannot tell you how much fun I had writing this play, particularly the third act.

When it was finished, I felt that I had a good fit for regional dinner theaters, which were then quite popular, if not Broadway.

One can always dream....

I circulated the script to several people in the industry whose opinions I respected, and the feedback was mostly positive. Abe Vigoda, then a publicity client and looking for a new stage vehicle to take to New York, expressed a definite interest in playing the lead. First, however, he wanted to attend a staged reading to see how *Hail on the Chief!* played for an audience.

For the most part, the rough staging at Lonny Chapman's Group Repertory Theatre went well. The actors did not carry scripts. They performed in front of the set for the theater's current production with a minimum of props and costumes.

Unfortunately, the two actors cast as the Secret Service agents played their roles too low-key, and it was often difficult to hear what they were saying. On the other hand, once other actors appeared on stage, the production came to life, bringing forth the response I had hoped for from the full house, filled with professional actors and writers. I was particularly pleased with the non-stop laughter the Micronesians elicited in the third act.

Hail on the Chief!, nevertheless, went nowhere after that reading. Abe Vigoda went on to other projects, as did I, and the script went back onto the shelf.

I would revisit it twice over the next several years. In the first instance, former client Pat Harrington (*One Day at a Time*), who was then performing in dinner theaters around the country, took an interest in the play and, over several weeks, we tightened and reworked parts of the script, but we disagreed on one or two major plot points, which ended (amicably) that collaboration.

I think that most professional writers will agree that collaboration works best when both writers are on the project from the start. Otherwise, the original writer, even if he sought his collaborator's help, considers him to be a bit of an interloper and tends to be overly protective of his "baby". To a certain extent, I was guilty of that.

Conversely, it *is* the original writer's "baby," and if he doesn't think that a particular change is right for his work, then he should not accept it. Once again: At the end of the day, it's going to be his name on that script, too.

One of the first things that I learned working in the entertainment business was that, when it comes to business, technical and, in my case, musical decisions, one should listen to the advice of people who are more knowledgeable in those areas than you. However, when you have to decide something that is purely artistic, you should go with your gut, because you are going to have to live with that decision. Yes, you may still fail, but that failure will be even more tragic if you instinctively knew the right path and didn't follow it.

If first time filmmaker Orson Welles had listened to the experts who told him, "You can't do that because it isn't done that way," would we have *Citizen Kane*? I don't think so.

I think that part of the reason *Hail on the Chief!* never really "flew" is because I ignored my own advice.

A couple of years after the Harrington collaboration ended, Mark Lonow, owner of The Comedy Club in Hollywood, took a brief interest in my play. I'd met Mark socially, and when I heard that he might be staging new plays at his facility, I called him. He asked me to send him a copy of the script.

Mark liked the play, but he insisted on some rewrites. Essentially, he wanted to bring the Micronesians on stage much earlier than their sole appearance in the third act.

I wasn't comfortable with that. I recalled to him the character of "Banjo" from one of the greatest of all American comedies, *The Man Who Came to Dinner*, played by Jimmy Durante in the 1941 movie version. On stage, like with my Micronesians, Banjo is discussed from time-to-time throughout the play, but the audience never sees him until the third act when his appearance totally invigorates the proceedings.

The Micronesians were my "Banjo," and I felt that bringing them on earlier would lessen their comic impact. But, since Mark was a potential producer, I did what he asked.

The new scenes I wrote were "cute" and Mark seemed to like them, but the possible production never went forward. Indeed, I'm not sure if he did any other plays at his club.

I would not revisit *Hail on the Chief!* again until 2005.

Even though I have no real musical abilities and can barely carry a tune, I love Broadway-style musicals. Back in the mid-1980s, in fact, I did try my hand at writing some lyrics, which Grammy-winning composer Michael Silvershur set to music. The songs were never commercially recorded, but the professionals who did hear them liked my lyrics. They said they were "literate" (i.e. they told a story) and were probably more suited for a book musical than a pop record.

I had always wanted to write an original musical comedy. True, *Jolson* and *Chevalier* were both musicals, but they were "juke box musicals," their complete scores made up from the songs that Al Jolson and Maurice Chevalier had made famous. I wanted to create something from scratch. *Almost scratch.*

The basis of my work was going to be *Hail on the Chief!*, which I thought would transform well into a musical. I would adapt my original play into a new book, and I would also write the song lyrics, a job I felt quite capable of handling.

To supply the music for my "literate" lyrics, I chose my son, David, who *is* a talented composer and musician. He was hesitant to accept the assignment at first, since his music preference is Rock, rather than Broadway musicals, but after some prodding, he agreed to do it.

David did make one suggestion. He felt that the play should be updated; that the Ronald Reagan/Gene Autry President should be changed to a character suggesting action movie star and California's then-current governor, Arnold Schwarzenegger.

I liked that idea and I went along with it, though I now tend to regret my decision, primarily because it made the play *too* topical.

"Topical" material becomes dated all too quickly.

I also made one other basic adjustment to the new book. The stage play had only one female character in it, the hero's girl friend. In a musical however, more female voices were needed, so I made one of the two Secret Service agents (the non-paranoid one) a woman. That change was a big plus, allowing for several humorous moments.

Over the next few months, David and I worked quite well together. I would e-mail him a lyric, tell him what kind of sound it should have, and he always seemed to come up with the right tune. It was a happy time for me, creating this show with my son.

With the help of singers Cindy Robinson and Matt Gould, we recorded a pretty good demo of the score. David supplied the music via his digital multi-track recorder and sang several of the roles on the recording. I even supplied the voice for the delusional king from Micronesia. Thankfully, for both the listener and myself, very little was required musically from this character and, for what there was, I could talk/sing it.

Were they still with us, neither Rex Harrison nor Richard Burton would have anything to worry about.

My wife, Sandy, and I had been planning to fly to Boston with her sons, Eric and Craig, to watch Craig run in the Boston Marathon, after which the two of us would spend a few days in New York City. I had never been to Boston and Sandy had never been to New York, so this was an opportunity to show the respective cities to each other. Naturally, since we were going to be in New York, I brought a dozen CDs of the *Hail on the Chief!* score with me.

While we were there, we met with producer Hy Juter, my friends, Abe Vigoda and George Dickerson, as well as some other key theatre people with whom we left a copy of the CD. The overall response to the project was positive, but Juter and others counseled that, if it was to move forward, we needed to do a staged reading of this new musical in front of an audience.

Everything was put "on hold" when we returned to Los Angeles. About a month after we got home, Sandy underwent the first of three back operations (over an eighteen month period), which resulted in her forced retirement from work. But, in 2007, I decided to move ahead and foot the bill for a three night staged reading of *Hail on the Chief!* at the prestigious Stella Adler Theatre on Hollywood Boulevard.[1]

I asked Jim Alexander, who I'd met when *Jolson* had been done at the Florida Studio Theatre in Sarasota, to direct. Together we held an open casting session that garnered us several talented people to join previously cast Bruce Kimmel (*The First Nudie Musical*), Bridget Hanley (*Here Come the Brides*) and Jim's wife, Broadway and voice (*Betty Boop*) actress Cindy Robinson, who had helped us with the show's original demo recording. There would be two full weekend days of rehearsals, with three evening performances the following Monday, Tuesday and Wednesday.

About a week before the rehearsals were to begin, I received a phone call from a friend of Cindy's. Jim was dead, the victim of a heart attack that morning while in the shower.

Once the initial shock had passed, I had a decision to make: Do I cancel the reading, or try to salvage what I had and move forward?

Jim Alexander was a professional. He would have wanted the show to go on, so that's the course I took.

My first problem was finding a new director. Had this been a straight play, I would have had no qualms about stepping into that role myself. Certainly I had plenty of experience as a stage director, and there was nobody who knew the material better than me. But, this was a musical, and there was absolutely no way that I was going to tackle that.

I phoned Gene Castle, who had directed and choreographed shows both on and off Broadway. We had talked once before about my project, but he'd been unavailable. After I explained to him my situation, he agreed to step in (for an exceptionally friendly fee) and stage the reading.

Some casting adjustments were also required. Obviously, Cindy Robinson was not going to do the show now, so I replaced her with Lisa Robert, a talented, quite likable performer, who we'd originally cast in the chorus. Another actor, a good friend of Jim's, also dropped out and Gene brought in Barry Pearl (*Grease*) to replace him.

---

1. Back in the day, the Stella Adler Theatre had been the location of a popular speakeasy frequented by the likes of Charlie Chaplin and W.C. Fields.

Miraculously, the reading, which was dedicated to the memory of Jim Alexander, came together, though the audience for the first night sat there virtually silent and never cracked a smile. "Depressed" does not come close to expressing how I felt when that performance had ended.

However, the second night was the total opposite. The audience laughed at virtually every joke, and they seemed to enjoy all of the songs. The final night was pretty much the same. I took the cast out to dinner after that final show had ended.

Although I was generally pleased with the experience, the three readings had made apparent several weaknesses in *Hail on the Chief!* that would have to be addressed if it was ever going to graduate to a professional production.

One of the first things that I did was to revise the book, sharpening some of the dialogue and eliminating a major subplot, which cut about ten or fifteen minutes off of the show's running time.

I then met with Bruce Kimmel, a master at developing and doctoring musicals. He felt that both the songs and the book needed further work, and he offered to help with both, and also direct a second staged reading of *Hail on the Chief!* for a fee.

Sandy and I discussed the matter. Since nobody had stepped forward after the three initial staged readings to finance a full production, we agreed to bring Bruce aboard. David was a bit reluctant at first, but he went along with the plan.

Off and on, Bruce and I worked together on the musical for about a year. During that time, he would briefly stop and do other short-term projects, as would I. It was also in the course of that year that Sandy's parents died and we, subsequently, decided to move to Austin, Texas.

During our collaboration, Bruce definitely improved the show's existing songs tenfold, while still remaining true to my original lyrics and David's music. He also wrote a couple of new numbers, including a wonderful first act finale. I couldn't have been happier with the contributions he made to the music and lyrics aspects of *Hail on the Chief!*

Where I disagreed with him was the book. Yes, he did give me some excellent ideas, which I incorporated but, for the most part, he insisted I cut a lot of dialogue that I felt worked and he didn't. However, since this was a musical and he was the expert, I ignored my gut feelings and went along with him.

Do not misunderstand. Bruce is a magnificent talent; terrific at what he does. He is also my friend, and a great wit. But, at least as far as *Hail on the Chief!* was concerned, our senses of humor were not in sync. And, it is virtually impossible for collaborators who are not on the same page humor-wise to come up with material that is funny.

The second staged reading of *Hail on the Chief!* was held (for two nights) at the Stella Adler about a year after the initial event. With three exceptions, the entire cast was different, populated by some superb performers that Bruce had brought in. Indeed, they were all sensational, as were most of the music and lyrics. But, the book just lay there. There were very few laughs during either performance.

Yes, I was extremely depressed when it was over, but I did take the cast out to dinner.

What to do next?

I still believed in this project, but since Sandy and I were now fully committed to moving to Austin and were even having a house built for us there, everything had to be put "on hold" once again.

My overall plan was to rework the book of *Hail on the Chief!*, going back to pretty much the revised version I'd done before I'd started working with Bruce. I would also keep all of the music/lyric work that Bruce had come up with and, with his help, record a new demo of the score with multiple singing voices, a fairly expensive undertaking. After that, I would try to set up a full production of the show. Possibly in Austin?

Truthfully, I don't think that a staged reading serves this particular material well, primarily because much of the humor is visual, and that is difficult to pull off when the actors are reading from scripts.

Most of my plan for the rebirth of *Hail on the Chief!* had to wait until after Sandy and I moved to Austin, which happened in April of 2009. Sadly, by the time we got settled in our new home and I was ready to get back to work on the project, outside events had intervened.

Arnold Schwarzenegger was not only out of office, but he was also involved in a well-publicized scandal. Thus, the timing would definitely not be right to proceed with the play...unless the characteristics of the "neighbor/President" were reworked, both in the book and several of the numbers. Such is the problem in dealing with topical subjects.

Perhaps another year went by before I decided that, as much as I loved the songs David, Bruce and I had written, perhaps a musical version of *Hail on the Chief!* was just not in the cards. Frankly, at seventy-one, I didn't feel like investing any more money into developing it.

Yet, I still felt that I had something special with the straight play version. Drawing the best material from both my original play and the musical, I revised the Schwarzenegger character to make him less recognizable, punched up some of the gags, and the three act comedy version of *Hail on the Chief!*, as well as *Putz*, have now been published in both paperback and Kindle editions. They are also available for production in any theater that wishes to license them them, and just recently *Hail on the Chief!* has been licensed by the Colonial Radio Theatre on the Air for a full cast audio dramatization that will be released in 2014… just in time for the mid-term elections.

21

The Publisher

BACK IN THE EARLY 1970S when I first started writing books, the idea of self-publishing was unthinkable.

There were plenty of legitimate publishers then, big and small, hardback and paperback, so if your writing was halfway decent and the subject of your work, fact or fiction, had some sort of commercial value, finding a publishing house to take it on (with or without an advance) might take time, but eventually your manuscript would find a home. Nobody but a "no-talent loser" would even think of publishing their own book, and those that did usually wound up with a garage filled with copies that they gave away to family, friends, acquaintances, passersby or anybody else who would take one.

Actually, one of these "no-talent losers" was my client, revered three-time Oscar-winning lyricist Paul Francis Webster, who had written a novel and, before discussing his decision with me, had contracted with a subsidy publisher to put out his book. "Why would you do that?" I asked him when he showed me the finished book. "You're Paul Francis Webster. You could have gotten a major publisher to do your novel, and they would have paid you an advance."

"I just wanted to see it in print," he said.

I guess I could have argued the point, but what would have been the sense of it? The book had been published. Sadly, because it was a self-published work, despite my efforts as a publicist, I was unable to secure any reviews or news stories about the book. Stores didn't stock it and sales were little or nothing.

On the other hand, had it been a non-fiction work that dealt with a subject of interest to a large enough segment of the reading public, Webster's book might have had a chance. Non-fiction is always an easier sell to both the public and the press than fiction, unless, of course, the author is Stephen King, James Patterson or the like.

One fiction writer that I did represent successfully was Ib Melchior, son of Lauritz Melchior, the revered opera singer. Ib not only wrote the short story that later became the basis for the cult classic *Death Race 2000* (1975) with David Carradine, but he also authored a series of World War II novels (e.g. *The Watchdogs of Abaddon, Eva*) that drew upon his experiences as a military intelligence investigator attached to the Counter Intelligence Corps during and after the war.

Both of the thrillers that I publicized for Ib had intriguing hooks that attracted press interviewers. One was built around the premise that Hitler had an illegitimate son and the other's concept was that Eva Braun did not die in the bunker with Hitler, but had escaped.

My first eight books were non-fiction, all published by legitimate, albeit medium-sized or small, publishers who paid me an advance for each one. The first seven dealt with Hollywood, movies and movie stars, and the eighth was a "How to" book, *The Art of Storytelling* (1997), which continues to sell extremely well and, as I already said, has been used as a text in college writing courses.

I had retained the publishing rights to my original screenplay of *Cheyenne Warrior* (1993), and based on the success of that movie, The Center Press agreed to publish it in book form. Over the next few years, they also published my two novels, *Nobody Drowns in Mineral Lake* (1999) and *Shadow Watcher* (2007).

However, by the time that *Shadow Watcher* came out, the book publishing industry had remarkably changed. Not only were readers making more and more book purchases through Amazon and other discounted on-line retailers, but the e-book was starting to become fashionable. Brick-and-mortar bookstores with their high overhead costs were also beginning to slowly disappear. Indeed, within the next decade or less, I believe that the only brick-and-mortar bookstores that will remain are those dealing with specialty subjects or used books.

Certainly the most revolutionary change in publishing was the invention of the inexpensive print-on-demand (POD) process. Now, a publisher could avoid printing thousands (or even hundreds) of copies of a particular title, but print them one-by-one as a customer purchased them. No longer would these publishers be stuck with cartons of books that did not sell.

The one problem with POD was that these books were "non-returnable," which meant that bookstores would be reluctant to stock them or even order them for an author signing. On the other hand, as book sales continue to skyrocket with Internet retailers in both physical and e-book copies, this particular disadvantage will dissipate.

Although, as of this writing, I have yet to actually see it, I have been informed that there will soon be a process whereby a reader can go into a store, order a particular book off the Internet, and have it printed and bound while they wait. With that method of distribution, who needs "returnability"?

My first self-publishing experience was with my book *Once Upon a Time in Hollywood: From the Secret Files of Harry Pennypacker* (2009).

This spoof of Hollywood's Golden Age and the tabloid press that covered it was filled with outrageous tall tales about John Wayne, Elvis Presley, Marilyn Monroe, Clark Gable, James Dean and other Hollywood icons, and also *The Wizard of Oz*. I had originally conceived it as a mockumentary movie, but when I was unable to raise the financing (*not even a nickel.*), I decided to expand my screenplay into a book.

I was sixty-eight at the time, did not have an agent and, considering the bizarre humor in this work, I figured that it might take an inordinate period of time to find representation and for them, in turn, to place the book with a publisher. I decided that I didn't want to wait.

A few of my friends had recently had good experiences with POD self-publishing. The fees they had paid were affordable, the encounters with the editors and book designers were satisfying and they'd been pleased with the finished product. "It really depends on the publisher that you go with," was the general consensus.

The most important thing that an author has to remember when he decides to self-publish is that, if he wants to sell books, he is going to have to promote the book himself. Then again, unless you are a well-known author with a major publisher, that's going to be the case anyway. A publisher might supply you with review copies and give you some ideas, but beyond that, publicizing or advertising your book is going to be up to you.

Of course, as a veteran author and publicist, promoting my own book was not an issue. I had had plenty of experience in that area.

For *Once Upon a Time in Hollywood*, I hired artist Dave Woodman to both design the cover and to also provide eight Al Hirschfeld-like caricatures of the different deceased movie stars who were the subjects of the lampoon. These drawings, rather than photographs, would not only be more fun and in keeping with the character of the book, but by using them I would avoid any possible "right of publicity" claims by the estates of these film icons.

I hired Wheatmark, an Arizona company, to design and publish the book, and I was quite pleased with both the working relationship and the finished product. The book is available in paperback, on Kindle and also in an audio version, narrated by Scott O'Neill.

Thanks to my promotion efforts, which included a book trailer that I wrote and directed myself, *Once Upon a Time in Hollywood* has sold well. It may not have made any best seller lists, but it continues to sell regularly more than three years after its publication, and people who have read it (and get the joke) seem to enjoy it.

As one lady said to me after finishing the book: "This is the biggest piece of bullshit I've ever read, but I couldn't stop laughing."

But, the reaction that really gets me is: "Are these stories true?"

As I said in a previous chapter, that why, these days, when I sign a copy of *Once Upon a Time in Hollywood*, I always precede my signature with: "Don't believe everything you read."

BearManor Media, a non-subsidy POD publisher specializing in books dealing with the entertainment industry, published my first memoir, *My Forty-Five Years in Hollywood and How I Escaped Alive* (2010) and, a year later, their fiction division (BearManor Fiction) published *Dracula Meets Jack the Ripper & Other Revisionist Histories*, my book of short stories. In 2011, they also re-published my 1975 book, *Basil Rathbone: His Life and His Films*, which had been out-of-print for thirty-five years.

I like working with BearManor. They strive to make their authors happy, which is why they are also publishing this book.

Manuscript copies of *The Hollywood Legends*, my eight one-person plays[1], had always been available for purchase on one of my websites. Oc-

---

1. *Clara Bow*, (Maurice) *Chevalier*, (Errol) *Flynn*, (Clark) *Gable*, (Al) *Jolson*, (Carole) *Lombard*, (Spencer) *Tracy* and *Orson Welles* were the original plays in the collection, but since I began writing this book, I've completed and published a ninth and tenth work, a two-person "juke box musical" play, *Nelson and Jeanette*, which deals with "American's Singing Sweethearts," Jeanette MacDonald and Nelson Eddy, plus another full length monologue, (Basil) *Rathbone*. All ten plays are also available together in a single volume, *The Hollywood Legends*.

casionally, I would sell a copy of one of them and, from time-to-time, I would license a stage production.

I knew there had to be a better way to market these plays to performers and theaters, but I had yet to find that avenue.

Then, in 2011, I became aware of Amazon's CreateSpace, a POD publishing arm of the Internet giant. Assuming you could maneuver your way through the template they supplied, this company makes it possible for you to turn your manuscript into an incredibly professional-looking paperback book for virtually nothing, then for a modest fee, makes it available for sale via Amazon and other retailers, as well as to libraries, throughout the United States, Canada, the United Kingdom and Europe. Author royalties are quite generous and, assuming sales meet a low minimum threshold, payable monthly.

CreateSpace, I figured, could be the answer to my dilemma.

I knew I wasn't going to get rich selling copies of my plays on Amazon or other retail sites. Actors, looking for a monologue to perform in class or as a showcase, might buy them, but the frosting on the cake would be the wide exposure the plays would get on Amazon. That could very well lead to a theater(s) deciding to stage one of them, and that's where I would make some decent money.

With my lack of design skills, I'm not sure if I would try formatting a novel or even a non-fiction book (with pictures) within the template supplied by CreateSpace, but I found that generating a simple "Acting Edition" with their mock-up was not a difficult task. Once I got the hang of it, it would take me less than a day to format each script, after which I would print out a copy for proof-reading, then upload the corrected PDF file to the CreateSpace website, which also gave me a simple method of generating an attractive cover. Once they approved everything and I approved everything, the book would be available for sale on Amazon (and elsewhere) within a week, if that long.

I also discovered that by simply converting my original Word files into the htm format, I could then upload them to Amazon's Kindle site, making the plays available as e-books. Frankly, I didn't think that I would make any sales on Kindle because I didn't think that people liked to *read* stage plays, but since it wasn't going to cost me anything to add this new potential sales venue, why not?

Bottom line: I was totally wrong. Not only do the plays sell extremely well every month in both editions, but the Kindle version outsells the paperback copies three or four to one. And, I've even licensed productions of some titles to theatre groups in different cities around the country.

Near the end of 2011, I came across an advertisement in one of the Hollywood trade papers, placed by screenwriter Alan Trustman (*The Thomas Crown Affair, Bullitt*). He had utilized CreateSpace to individually publish six of his unproduced screenplays under the collective title of *Six Great Unproduced Screenplays*. The purpose of the ad, I presume, was to attract the attention of filmmakers who might produce them.

Every professional screenwriter has spec scripts sitting on his shelf that did not sell, or if they did sell, they were never produced.

In fact, I'll go so far to say that for most of us "schmucks with Underwoods," as mogul Jack Warner used to refer to his studio writers, for every produced credit on our résumé, there are two or three screenplays that are gathering dust.

That doesn't necessarily mean that these are not well written scripts or engrossing stories. There are many reasons why a good screenplay might not be produced, financing and timing being at the top of the list. Or, it might be that that particular script was never presented to or read by the "right person".

I've had a good career as a screenwriter, so I'm not really complaining. But, what has always been disheartening is the fact that a few of my unsold scripts represent some of my best work as a writer. The stories and characters are viable and it saddens me that I've not had the opportunity to share them with the public.

In one instance, I converted my original screenplay into a novel (*Shadow Watcher*), while with three others, I adapted them into short stories, and they can be found in my book, *Dracula Meets Jack the Ripper & Other Revisionist Histories*.

Nevertheless, there were several other unsold scripts that I felt had merit, and if a major screenwriter like Alan Trustman was going to self-publish his work, why should I be reluctant to do the same?

Although it would definitely be nice to see one or more of my scripts actually produced, *my* underlying goal was different that Trustman's. I just wanted people to read my stories. After all, as I said in the Preface, a good story is a terrible thing to waste.

The only real question was: Would the public be interested in reading these stories in screenplay form, particularly if it was an *unproduced* screenplay?

The answer is: Yes and No.

All of the screenplays have sold, some much better than others. But none of them have done as well as the stage plays, which (*fingers crossed*) sell continually, month after month. Since the plays deal with famous movie stars, they seem to have a built-in audience.

For the record, the scripts in the screenplay series, collectively titled *Read a Movie!* are:

Barry & the Bimbo (an action/romantic comedy)

Black Watch / The Cavern (two screenplays in one book, one a action/horror film set in Scotland's Edinburgh Castle, and the other a science-fiction alien creature tale that takes place in Virginia's Luray Caverns)

Charla (a personal drama, inspired by my time with actress Charla Doherty)

Ghoul City (a horror/black comedy)

Matricide (a mystery-thriller, inspired by the murder of my former client, actress Susan Cabot)

Ride Along (an action/romantic comedy)

Sarah Golden Hair (a Western, and perhaps the best script I've ever written)

The Summer Folk (a nostalgic, semi-autobiographical family drama)

Uncle Louie (a family coming-of-age comedy that I wrote for my friend and client, Abe Vigoda).

Also, since I had retained the publishing rights, I packaged the two unproduced versions of the *Cheyenne Warrior* sequel that I had written for Roger Corman and published them as *Cheyenne Warrior II / Hawk*. Not surprisingly, this book and *Sarah Golden Hair* are the two best sellers of all these published screenplays.

Having just recently added my two multiple character stage plays, *Hail on the Chief!* and *Putz* (both talked about in the previous chapter) to my list of CreateSpace published titles, my shelf of *worthwhile* forgotten, dust-covered scripts is now bare. My ignored "children" are now out in the world for the public to read and, if luck will have it, theaters and film-makers to produce.

I guess that, after I finish this book, I'm just going to have to write something else *new*.

22

Autograph Shows

I DISCOVERED AUTOGRAPH SHOWS virtually by accident.

I was researching my one-person play about Orson Welles; trying to locate an old copy of *Playboy Magazine* that contained an in-depth interview with the filmmaker. A friend (Woody Wise) told me about this event, an autograph show that was being held in North Hollywood at The Beverly Garland Hotel. He said that there would be many dealers present who sold old magazines.

It cost me five dollars to get into the show and, once inside, I discovered that not only was the place filled with dealers in old magazines, vintage autographs, posters and other movie memorabilia, but there were a half-dozen rows of tables in the "ballroom" at which sat perhaps seventy-five actors and actresses, all former stars or familiar faces from movies and television. Some of these folk (e.g. Robert Horton, Gary Lockwood) were former publicity clients that I hadn't seen in years.

All of these celebrities had stacks of 8x10 photographs in front of them, which they were there to sign *and sell* to the eager fans that wanted to meet them.

For years, movie and television stars had freely given their autographs to any fan who had asked for them. Some of these fans could be quite demanding and intrusive. They would not only interrupt the celebrity's meal when he/she was eating in a restaurant, but occasionally one would also follow them into the restroom in order to get a signature.

This kind of rude behavior can sometimes be tolerated, but there was a certain segment of fans that really took unfair advantage of the graciousness of the celebrities. These "fans" were, in fact, autograph dealers, who would obtain the star's signature, then sell it for a nice profit.

Back in the 1970s, I recall sitting with my client, Howard Keel, at a public screening of his film, *Kiss Me Kate*. This was first time the classic musical had been shown in 3-D since its initial release, and several people involved in the production were in attendance.

After the screening, many people approached Howard for an autograph, which he was happy to give them, but there was one wiry, bespectacled fellow who caught my eye. He was standing off to the side with an armful of record albums, VHS tapes and photographs. Howard was chatting with other people, so he didn't pay much attention to this guy who, every now and then, would sidle up to him and have him sign just one of his items. By the time the evening was over, this dealer probably had fifteen-twenty items, with signatures that cost him nothing, which he would later sell.

Autograph shows changed all of that. Now, the celebrities benefited from the sale of their signatures and, as in the case of many of these former stars whose careers had either stalled or ended, these events not only provided them with a new source of revenue, but they also gave them the opportunity to connect with fans who had not forgotten them.

Most of the celebrities at these events do well and walk away with a thousand dollars or much more in cash in their pockets. On the other hand, others surprisingly don't. I recall attending a show where one of the guests was actor-folk singer Theodore Bikel (*The Defiant Ones*, *My Fair Lady*), who I don't believe sold a single autograph. As he was packing up to leave, he commented, "I guess these people don't know who I am, or who I used to be."

Incidentally, I was unable to find that *Playboy Magazine* with the Orson Welles interview at that first autograph show I attended, but awhile later I found a guy in the San Fernando Valley who said he had a copy that he would sell to me for fifty cents.

When I arrived at his three-bedroom house, I could not believe what I saw.

Two of the bedrooms, as well as a good part of his living room, were filled with long tables with boxes of magazines sitting atop them.

We're not talking *Life, Time, Ladies Home Journal, Popular Mechanics* or even comic books.

This fellow seemed to have every issue (and sometimes multiple copies) of *Playboy, Hustler* and virtually every other girlie (also porno) magazine ever published.

If you wanted it, he had it.

He found the *Playboy* I was looking for. Silently wishing I was wearing rubber gloves, I quickly made sure that the Welles interview was intact, paid him the fifty cents and left.

When I got home, I took a shower.

Before the advent of celebrity autograph shows, movie and television personalities would be hired by the promoters of car shows, store openings or rodeos in various cities in the United States and Canada to be an extra-added attraction at their event. The celebrity would be paid a flat fee plus expenses to fly to these weekend shows and sign 8x10 photographs for a set number of hours each day. The promoter would pay for the photos, which would be given free to the fans.

When Steve Kanaly was co-starring on the *Dallas* television series, we attended several of these events together, sometimes averaging one per month, two or three months in a row. As his publicist, I was there to collect any monies owed and to make sure that he was treated properly.

There were certainly some memorable moments during those trips.

I think it was in Lafayette, Louisiana, that we walked into a restaurant one evening for dinner. A gorgeous brunette strolled out of the bar, spotted Steve and walked over to him. "You're mine tonight," she said in her sultry voice.

Steve maneuvered away from her, pointed to me and said, "I want you to meet my friend, Michael Druxman."

The woman stared daggers at me, and said, "I know what you are to him."

To this very day, I have no idea what she thought I was to him.

In Wichita, Kansas, I encountered a different kind of tricky situation.

After one bad experience with a promoter who cancelled a gig the day before we were supposed to fly to his event, Steve and I agreed that any future personal appearances would have to be firmed with a non-refundable deposit of half the agreed upon fee, payable upon booking. The balance would be paid, via a cashier's check, upon our arrival in the designated city and before Steve appeared at the event itself.

We arrived in Wichita late Friday afternoon and, as we were being driven to our hotel, we were informed that the balance of the fee would be waiting for us on Saturday at the car show. At the event, the promoter invited us up to his office where not only was his wife present, but also a couple of big, rather rough-looking truck driver types who were there conducting some sort of business.

In front of these two guys who, despite their daunting appearances, may very well have been the most honest people in the world, the promoter handed me an envelope containing the balance of the fee, several thousand dollars *in cash*.

I looked at the guys. They were eyeing the envelope.

I looked at Steve, and he didn't appear to be too happy with the situation either.

"I thought you were going to give me a cashier's check," I said to the promoter.

"I didn't have time to get to the bank," he said.

I looked back at the guys. Though they'd turned away slightly, they were still watching the envelope.

There was no way that I was going to leave that office and walk around for the next two days with that envelope full of cash.

"You keep the cash," I said to the promoter. "Write me a personal check."

He did. The check cleared. And, I didn't wind up in a dark Wichita alley with my head bashed in.

One of the most enjoyable jaunts that Steve and I took together was to Halifax, Nova Scotia, where I not only enjoyed the most sensational fish dinner I've ever had in my life, but while we were there the captain of a British submarine invited us to tour his vessel while it was in port. It was quite a kick looking through the periscope, and I couldn't stop myself. I just had to shout, "Fire One!"[1]

The trip back to Los Angeles on Sunday night was *not* fun. The connecting flight out of Chicago encountered lightning, thunder and major turbulence. Aside from Steve and myself, other passengers in first class included Sorrell Brooke and Rick Hurst (both from *The Dukes of Hazzard*), who had been doing car shows that weekend in other Canadian cities, and, sitting next to me, Joe Esposito, a close friend of the late Elvis Presley and the road manager for Michael Jackson, John Denver and others.

During that edgy flight, I couldn't help thinking that, should the plane go down, it would be the worst airline disaster in show business history.

---

1. For all you fans of submarine movies, be advised that these underwater ships are extremely cramped. There is no way that John Wayne, Clark Gable, Burt Lancaster or any other 6' star could have effortlessly maneuvered around inside those vessels, let alone fit through the top hatch.

Thankfully, nobody had to read that headline, but since you're reading this book, I guess you've already figured that out yourself.

Although I was then making my living writing screenplays for Roger Corman and others and wasn't doing publicity any longer, during the late 1990s, I started booking former clients into these autograph shows. I didn't do it so much for the commission that I earned off their sales. I enjoyed the interaction with the other people who were there, old friends and clients that I hadn't seen in a long time, and also actors and directors whose work I'd admired for years and who I finally got the opportunity to meet and, in many cases, get to know rather well.

Among the people I booked and worked with at these shows were Steve Kanaly, Diane McBain, Bridget Hanley, Pato Hoffmann (from *Cheyenne Warrior*), Michael Ansara, Dan O'Herlihy and even Roger Corman.

With Michael Ansara and Dan O'Herlihy, I had to almost force them at gunpoint to appear at the show, but when it was over and they saw how much money they'd earned from selling their signed photos, both were eager to do the event again.

A few months before I moved to Austin, Texas, in 2009, I even appeared as a guest at one of these events, and I did quite well selling my recently published book, *Once Upon a Time in Hollywood: From the Secret Files of Harry Pennypacker*. In fact, that experience made me realize that, if one picks the right venue, a writer will sell many more books at these kinds of gatherings, rather than at standard book store signings.

Since 2009, I have done two autograph shows in Chicago[2], as well as a pair of comic conventions in Austin, plus horror movie conventions in Dallas and Los Angeles. I sold many books (and DVDs) at all of these shows, but none was more successful than the Dallas appearance where my sales more than doubled any place else. I'm sure that my Roger Corman connection and the horror-sci-fi films I did for him had something to do with that.

These shows are tiring to do, but they can also be quite gratifying, particularly when a fan who has read one of your books or seen a film you've written, approaches your table and either buys your latest offering, or asks you to sign the slipcase of their already owned VHS or DVD.

---

2. Being a devoted fan of the gangster film, as well as the writer of the original screenplay that became *Dillinger and Capone* (1995), the *real* reason why I wanted to go to Chicago was to visit the Biograph Theater, and the alley next to it where, in 1934, bank robber John Dillinger was shot down by the F.B.I.

For some reason that I can't fathom, *Raptor* (2001) seems to be the most requested slipcase for signature.

Not all of these events go well though.

I was booked for a show in Scottsdale, Arizona, and the promoter had agreed to take care of my hotel bill, supply ground transportation while there and also reimburse me for both my wife's and my airfare from Austin and back.

As is our custom, we arrived at the Austin airport more than an hour before our flight and, as we were checking our luggage, we were informed that the flight to Phoenix, which services Scottsdale, had been delayed four hours. That "four hours" would turn into more than seven.

I immediately phoned the promoter, who told me not to worry. I should call him just before our flight took off and he would have us met at the airport and taken to the hotel.

Sitting in the airport for almost seven hours did not make me a "happy camper." When the airline people informed us that our plane was now in flight from Dallas and less than an hour away, I phoned the promoter… only to discover than his "mailbox" was "full".

I then phoned the hotel where we were supposed to be staying and found out that there was no reservation for us and, although there *were* rooms available, *I* would have to pay for them. Also, there was no shuttle from the hotel, so if there was nobody at the airport to meet me, I would have to pay for a forty-five minute taxi ride to Scottsdale.

I made a decision and, as it turned out, it was a wise one.

"We're going home," I said to Sandy, my blood boiling. "We're not going to fly into Phoenix at ten o'clock at night and find ourselves stranded." We got our luggage off the plane and went home.

Next day, I got on the phone to the airline. Not only did they refund our plane fares (over nine hundred dollars) in full, but they also gave us four hundred dollars in flight vouchers because of the problem.

A few months later, I read some postings on Facebook by other people who had been promised reimbursements by the promoter. It seems that the checks he had given these people had bounced.

So, even though we missed the show itself, I guess with the flight vouchers, I came out ahead on that deal.

Without doubt, the most rewarding moment I've ever had at an autograph show was at the first comic convention I attended in Austin. It was near the end of the day on Sunday when a gentleman, probably in his early fifties and carrying a bag filled with signed photographs that he'd purchased from the various celebrities in attendance, approached my table and looked over the half dozen books I had for sale. He wound up purchasing a copy of every title, plus two extras of *The Art of Storytelling*.

As he walked away, he said to me, "Finally, I've found something here that's worthwhile."

23

Surviving in Austin

THIS IS THE MOST DIFFICULT CHAPTER in this book to write, primarily because it is the final one and it is supposed to bring my story up to date.

My problem is that, as soon as I finish this book and send it off to my publisher, I will probably start writing something else, and by the time you read this, it will no longer be current.

Life does have its difficult moments, doesn't it?

Although there are aspects about Los Angeles (e.g. my son, stepsons, friends, New York-style delicatessens, being able to borrow Academy Awards screeners from neighbors, etc.) that I sometimes miss, I do enjoy living in Austin, Texas.

For the most part, the people I've met in Texas are nice. I reside in a quiet, peaceful neighborhood where I can write or relax without being disturbed. I am no longer part of the Hollywood "rat race," and, surprisingly, I no longer feel the need to see every "hot" new movie as soon as it hits the theaters. Indeed, I have no problem waiting two or three months until it is released onto DVD and I can rent it at my local Blockbuster at the senior citizen rate.

When *My Forty-Five Years in Hollywood…And How I Escaped Alive* was published back in 2010, I flew back to Los Angeles for a few days in order to do a book signing and promote the work in other ways. We had been living in Austin for about eighteen months then.

As we drove off the parking lot in our rented car and headed into the traffic and smog-filled city, I turned to Sandy and said, "If we weren't here to see family and promote the book, I'd just turn around and take the next plane back to Austin."

My 2012 trip to Los Angeles to appear as a celebrity guest at a horror convention only reinforced that assessment.

On the other hand, Austin is not all that I expected, and there have been some disappointments.

When Sandy and I were making our plans to move here, people involved in local film and theatre operations continually gushed about how, with my show business background, there would be so many opportunities for me here. "You'll be one of only two 'script doctors' in Texas," I was told by a friend, a former personal manager in Hollywood, now a casting director in Austin.

I *have* had some well-paying screenwriting assignments since I've been in Austin, but they are gigs that I would have gotten anyway, since they came from producers in either Los Angeles or on the East Coast who had seen or read my previous work.

Also, once I discovered *iMovie* on my Mac, I put my publicist's hat back on again to produce a series of trailers for YouTube and other websites in order to promote my various writings. I am now being hired by fellow writers to do trailers for their books and also by singers and composers to create music videos. I love doing these mini-movies. They are simple to construct, and they keep my creative juices flowing.

Aside from these projects, the only real writing activity I've had in Austin was as the story editor for a local independent film producer. I worked out of my home office, reviewing and commenting on story outlines for movies that he was planning to make. The problem was that his ideas of what made a good (or even decent) story and my ideas did not mesh, so since I have never been a "Yes Man," we parted company after two or three weeks.

Beyond that short-term employment, I have kept busy in other ways, speaking to various groups (e.g. Lions Club, Network Austin Mixer, Sherlock Holmes Society, etc.), the autograph shows and, for the past two years, I've served as either a panelist or headed a series of roundtable discussions at the Austin Film Festival. I've even taught a class for the Texas Writer's League at St. Edwards University.

One thing that I definitely miss about living in Los Angeles is the *professional* show business ambiance; chatting with colleagues who have actually worked in Hollywood or New York, rather than just "brushed shoulders" with filmmakers when a Hollywood movie came to their town to shoot on location.

Yes, the *Dallas* television series filmed in Dallas, and both the 2010 *True Grit* remake and the *Friday Night Lights* television series were shot in Austin, but those were still Hollywood-based projects. Local talent may have played extras or filled secondary acting roles and crew assignments, but the key cast members and principal creative people came from either the West or East Coasts.

There is definitely a lot of superb talent in Austin, as well as in other parts of the country, but despite claims to the contrary, none of these places will ever become a professional filmmaking community until the actual financing, creative decisions and production/post-production activities for their motion pictures are generated within that particular state or community.

It's a simple matter of economics. Unless the person is a major star or the project is going to be shot on a distant location, why would a Hollywood-based production, particularly an episodic television series, cast somebody who lives in Austin, Chicago or wherever when there are probably dozens of local actors who can play that role just as well? And with them, the company doesn't have to pay for plane tickets, hotels and a per diem in order to bring these actors (or directors or writers) into town.

I even know a couple of well known actors who used to work regularly in episodic television and, occasionally, movies who, after they moved to the East Coast, found that there were few, if any, job offers emanating from Hollywood. Travel expenses had made casting them too costly.

As I always tell aspiring screenwriters, actors and directors that I meet at places where I speak: "If you want to have a *serious* career in motion pictures, then move to Los Angeles, because that's where the business is located."

How much I miss that professional show business ambiance became even more apparent to me when I did the 2012 horror convention in Los Angeles. Aside from visiting with old friends like Bridget Hanley and Bruce Kimmel, I also finally met actor Clu Gulager (*The Last Picture Show*, *The Virginian* television series). We seemed to have an immediate connection, probably because, like with Bridget and Bruce, we have experienced the *real* motion picture business.

Gulager and I have a couple of things in common. Not only were we both students at the University of Washington Drama Department (at different times), but we have both also played "Osric" in *Hamlet*. As noted in an earlier chapter, I did the role in a UW television production, and

Gulager played the part in a staging at Baylor University in which Burgess Meredith played "Hamlet" and Charles Laughton directed.

Clu recalled to me that, in preparing for the foppish role, he padded both his stomach and his bottom. During the initial dress rehearsal, after he had delivered his first line, Laughton stopped the run-through and asked, "Are you doing *me*?"

A few weeks before meeting Gulager, I had watched again the 1964 version of *The Killers*, in which he and Lee Marvin had played the title roles in the picture that had co-starred Angie Dickinson, John Cassavetes and, in his final film before entering the political arena, Ronald Reagan. Breakfasting in the hotel restaurant one morning of the convention, I asked Gulager if the subtext of his and Marvin's relationship in that movie was that they were a gay couple. Certainly, since the movie was released in 1964 before the Production Code was abandoned, a homosexual relationship would have to have been subtext.

"No," he said, "but that is a terrific idea. I wish I had thought of that then. I know that Lee would have gone along with that idea."

I do enjoy talking with fans, as well as aspiring actors, screenwriters and directors, but more than that, I like chatting with fellow professionals. We have shared a parallel path in life even though those paths may never have crossed.

One never knows what the future holds. There will probably be other conventions to attend, classes to teach and, hopefully, other writing assignments. I have found that, more often than not, opportunities suddenly appear when one least expects them.

Recently, for example, I've been enjoying myself, wearing my director's hat again, working with different actors to adapt some of my stage plays and other works into audio books. As I write this, not only is my book, *Once Upon a Time in Hollywood: From the Secret Files of Harry Pennypacker* available for download, but also *Dracula Meets Jack the Ripper and Other Revisionist Histories* (read by Fred Frees), *Shadow Watcher* (read by Alan Douglas) and, performed as a radio-style drama by Ed French, my one-person play. *Orson Welles*.

People I meet tell me that I've led an interesting life.

And, now that I think about it, I guess I have.

www.ingramcontent.com/pod-product-compliance
Lightning Source LLC
Chambersburg PA
CBHW071436150426
43191CB00008B/1149